SO-BNY-339
...ARY
...e
Denver, Colorado 80204

¡Viva!

RIGHT TO READ

# FAMOUS MEXICAN AMERICANS

Ann Fears Crawford
and
Pedro Chapa, Jr.

*Illustrated by Robert Palomo*

**Steck–Vaughn Company**
A Division of Intext
**Austin, Texas**

# TABLE OF CONTENTS

NOTICE: Answer Key is bound in the back of the book.

ISBN 0-8114-0513-3

Copyright © 1976 by Steck-Vaughn Company, Austin, Texas

All rights reserved. No part of this book may be reproduced in any form without the written permission of the publisher.
Printed and Bound in the United States of America

2 3 4 5 6 7 8 9 0 − 80 79 78 77

# INTRODUCTION

## Joe J. Bernal

Ann Fears Crawford and Pedro Chapa, Jr., have done a magnificent job in writing this timely book about very outstanding Americans—people we should know because they have set a good example for us to follow. All of them are Mexican Americans, Hispanos, Chicanos—*Mejicanos* all—and this is what makes the book timely.

For many years we have been reading about many outstanding Americans, but for a variety of reasons, few or none have been Mexican Americans. Some think it is because Mexican Americans do not make good citizens. Others think that writers do not know much about Hispanos. Still others are sure that it is because people discriminate against Chicanos. Whatever the reason or reasons may be, until recently little has been written about *Mejicanos*.

Indians and Spaniards were in America long before the Pilgrims landed at Plymouth Rock. Yet, most historians and writers would have you believe that the history of the Southwest began in 1821 when Stephen Austin and various Anglo families entered and settled in Texas. On the contrary, Indians had been living in that area and many other areas for over 25,000 years!

When we trace Indian life, we find they had many outstanding civilizations. One of the most spectacular of these civilizations was centered around Tenochtitlán, known today as Mexico City. Its pyramids were larger and better constructed than the pyramids of Egypt. Yet, many people recognize Egypt as the cradle of civilization.

The Spaniards came into the Southwest in 1528, seventy-nine years before the English landed in Virginia. Mexican Americans can be proud of the Indians and the Spaniards. Out of these two groups, the *mestizo* Mexican Americans were born. This book is about those people.

For many years the *Mejicanos* in the Southwest spoke and read Spanish. This was the language they knew best. After Texas's war for independence and the war between the United States and Mexico, the southwestern states of New Mexico, Arizona, Texas, Colorado, and California became part of the United States. In a sense two worlds developed: one in which people spoke English, and another where people spoke Spanish. Those who understood the two worlds were a lucky few. Most people existed in and understood only one.

In the United States today, most people speak English. History is written in that language, and the heroes are mainly Anglos. Many history books present just one side of the story. For example there is the story of the Mexican American revolutionist, Juan Nepomuceno Cortina, who was considered dangerous because, among other things, he could speak both languages. "Cheno," as Cortina was called, saw land being taken away from the Mexican Americans because they could not understand laws written in English. He attempted to protect them. He became a hero to many Mexican Americans, but to the English-speaking people, he was a *bandido*.

During World War I and World War II, *Mejicanos* left the *barrios* to defend American democracy on distant battlefields. They served well, and many returned home as highly decorated heroes.

As they had defended their country, so they returned ready to defend their civil rights at home.

After World War II, thousands of *Mejicanos* decided to improve their education. When President John F. Kennedy expressed a concern that many Americans were not finishing school, *Mejicanos* understood. As a result of this new push for education, many *Mejicanos* now not only speak English and Spanish, but read and write both languages as well.

As you read through the pages of this book, you will make some very dear friends—people who could be your neighbors. You will read about my favorite person, *"el obispo del barrio,"* Bishop Patrick Flores. He has been a fighter for civil rights, a raiser of funds for scholarships, a supporter of the farm workers, a *mariachi* singer, a jail chaplain, but most of all, a warm and concerned leader. You will also meet the person who has taught all Americans how callous our society has been in its disregard for the well-being of its farm workers—César Chávez. If you like sports, there is the great Stanford football star, Jim Plunkett, and "Super Mex," the light-hearted golf star, Lee Treviño. If you like *cuentos* (stories and ballads), meet the best in the Southwest—folklorist Américo Paredes, who can tell them, sing them, and write them!

You can also read about Mexican American women who have made their mark on American life. Take Florencia Bisenta de Casillas Martínez Cardona, better known to us as Vikki Carr. If she is not the best singer in the U.S., she is certainly among the best. You will meet attorney Grace Olivárez, the state planner of New Mexico. She was a GED recipient before she went to college. Lupe Anguiano is another proud Chicana. You'll find her a delight to know. Then there's "Chelo"—over seventy years old and at this tender age one of the best artists in Texas. There is also a Chicana who has worked hard to obtain her education and now helps others do the same, Mari-Luci Jaramillo.

You will also meet some civil rights leaders. José Ángel Gutiérrez has made a name for himself through his work with La Raza Unida party. Colorado citizens know Rodolfo "Corky" Gonzales as a boxer, poverty worker, poet-historian—and now a crusader for justice. Reies Tijerina has made history with his fight to help Chicanos in New Mexico regain their land rights. Read on and you'll also meet the tireless Doctor Héctor García, who founded a national veterans' organization, the GI Forum.

Mexican Americans have always had outstanding public servants. They are hard workers, committed to representing all their constituents. The team is led nationally by the outstanding New Mexico senator, Joseph Montoya, followed by the highly respected members of Congress, Edward R. Roybal of California and Henry B. González of Texas. Two state governors, Jerry Apodaca of New Mexico and Raul H. Castro of Arizona, are setting a great pace at the state level.

On the local scene, there is writer-historian Julián Nava, who is head of the Los Angeles school board. Read about the folk-singer who came out of the *barrios* of Dallas, Trini López. Get to know the man whose bluebonnet paintings have hung on the office walls of the presidents of the U.S. and Mexico, Porfirio Salinas.

These are great people; many of them are products of the *barrios* and quite proud of it. They have made many contributions and are still working to make America a better place to live and play and work.

# César Chávez

Life can be very hard if you are a farm worker toiling in the fields of the United States. Long hours, back-breaking labor, poor living conditions, and little pay are often all a farm worker can count on.

Some people have tried to free the farm workers from these conditions. One person, César Chávez, has come closer than anyone else to accomplishing this. The late Robert F. Kennedy called him "one of the heroic figures of our time."

César Chávez was born in 1927 on a farm in the Gila River Valley near Yuma, Arizona. His early years were comfortable and happy.

In 1937, however, his family felt the terrible effects of the Great Depression. Their farm had to be sold to pay debts. César's family moved to California to work in the fields.

Home was often the back of their old Studebaker car. Other times the family lived in labor camps. The children went to many schools. When César entered the seventh grade, he still could not read or write.

Working in the fields was very diffi-cult. "You stoop and dig, stoop and dig," César recalls. "It's work for an ani-mal, not for a person." One time the family worked for seven weeks, only to have their contractor disappear with their pay.

In 1939 the Chávezes were living in San Jose, California, in a *barrio* called *Sal si Puedes*, "escape if you can." A union tried to organize the workers in the dried fruit industry. César's father and uncle joined the union.

"They had a strike and my father and uncle picketed at night," César remembers. "It made a deep impression on me. But of course they lost the strike, and that was the end of the union."

César left home when he was in his teens. In Delano, California, he met Helen Fávila. By now César had a strong desire to do something to help the farm workers. Helen shared his dream. The two married and began to rear a family.

César and Helen returned to live with César's family in San Jose, California. Nine members of the family lived in one small house and worked in the fields.

César says, "We worked there for two and a half years. Later we figured the whole family together was making twenty-three cents an hour."

In 1952 César met Fred Ross of the Community Service Organization. The CSO, as the organization was called, helped Mexican Americans with their problems with the police, the immigration authorities, the welfare department, and other agencies.

Ross convinced César to join the CSO. For ten years César worked hard for this organization. In 1958 he became the director of the program.

However, César kept his dream of helping the farm workers. He wanted to organize a union solely for farm workers. When the CSO refused to help form this union, César quit.

He was offered another job at a very high salary. Instead, César and his family returned to Delano. There Helen worked picking grapes, while César knocked on doors trying to organize a union.

César talked to thousands of people. Many came to his house and stood in his front yard while he spoke.

The farm workers formed a union called the National Farm Workers Association. By 1965 it had over 1,700 members. The farm workers began to refer to their struggle as *La Causa*.

On September 16, Mexican Independence Day, the union members voted to join migrant Filipino grape pickers in a strike. The Filipino workers belonged to one of the AFL-CIO unions, and this union merged with Chávez's organization to form the United Farm Workers of America.

Robert Kennedy with César Chávez on the Day Chávez Ended His Fast

*La Huelga*, as the strike was called, lasted five years. It attracted much attention from magazines, newspapers, radio, and television.

One of the high points of the strike was a three-hundred-mile march César and some union members made to the capital of the state. Thousands of people joined for short marches along the way.

Soon several contracts were signed. The workers obtained better wages, a union hall, and paid vacations. The union had won its first victory.

These contracts were with wine-grape growers, however. Table-grape growers refused to sign. Chávez established a nationwide boycott of California grapes. People all across the country were asked not to buy grapes. At one time, the grape industry lost over 20 percent of its business.

The Famous March to Sacramento, California

Some of the striking farm workers wanted to use force to win their cause. César spoke out against violence. He decided to go on a fast for peace and nonviolence. He did not eat for twenty-five days. He lay on a cot at a garage in Delano.

Hundreds of people came to visit Chávez during the fast. When he ended his fast, a mass was celebrated. Ten thousand people attended, including the late Senator Robert Kennedy.

By 1970 more than 80 percent of the growers had signed contracts. Farm workers began to receive better wages. Many improvements in both living and working conditions were begun. At last farm workers began to notice some change in the quality of their lives.

The man most responsible for this is César Chávez. For this reason, he is greatly respected and loved by many people, especially the farm workers.

However, César feels that the struggle is not over. He says that much work remains to be done. César Chávez continues his long and difficult struggle for *La Causa*.

## A. UNDERSTANDING THE STORY

Read each of the following carefully. Then select the correct answer from the choices. Write the letter of the correct answer in the blank that follows each.

1. César's early childhood was (a) very unhappy, (b) spent working in the fields, (c) comfortable and happy. ............

2. During the Great Depression, César's family (a) was able to pay its debts, (b) sold its farm, (c) moved to California to work in a factory. ............

3. César first left San Jose (a) because he wanted to marry Helen Fávila, (b) when he was in his teens, (c) because he wanted to work for the CSO. ............

4. César joined the CSO and (a) immediately became director, (b) organized a union under the CSO program, (c) worked hard for ten years. ............

5. César's union was originally called the (a) National Farm Workers Association, (b) AFL-CIO, (c) United Farm Workers Association. ............

6. One of the high points of the strike was a (a) two-hundred-mile march to the state capital, (b) three-hundred-mile march to the United States capital, (c) three-hundred-mile march to the state capital. ............

7. The union's first contract was with (a) table-grape growers, (b) wine-grape growers, (c) all grape growers. ............

8. One of the reasons César fasted was to (a) help stop violence, (b) improve his health, (c) pray for victory. ............

9. By 1970 many growers (a) had lost over 20 percent of their business, (b) had signed contracts, (c) still refused to sign contracts.    ............

10. César feels that the farm worker's struggle (a) will never end, (b) is now finished, (c) is still not over.    ............

## B. VOCABULARY

Match each word in Column A with its meaning in Column B by writing the letter of the meaning in the blank in front of the word.

| | Column A | | Column B |
|---|---|---|---|
| ............ 1. | toiling | a. | act of not eating for a period of time |
| ............ 2. | debts | b. | to be on guard at a place where workers are striking |
| ............ 3. | strike | c. | working |
| ............ 4. | picket | d. | worth or fineness of a thing |
| ............ 5. | merge | e. | unite |
| ............ 6. | impression | f. | to bring up, to help grow up |
| ............ 7. | rear | g. | act of stopping work so as to obtain some demand |
| ............ 8. | fast | h. | an effect left upon the mind |
| ............ 9. | boycott | i. | money which a person owes |
| ............ 10. | quality | j. | refusing to buy or to use in order to obtain some demand |

## C. THINGS TO TALK ABOUT

Think about the following. Discuss them with your friends or other people you are studying with.

1. How did César feel about working in the fields? Do you know any people who feel the same way about their work? What can be done to prevent this?

2. Can you give examples that show César's dedication to the idea of helping farm workers?

3. What do you think of strikes and boycotts as a way to gain better wages and better working conditions?

4. What do you think of César's idea of nonviolence?

Photo by Adam Medrano

*Active Chicana*

# Lupe Anguiano

"Mexican American women must get out and change the world," says Lupe Anguiano. When she speaks, Mexican American women listen. Lupe is constantly challenging Mexican American women to be active in politics, their communities, and ethnic affairs. "Now our role is not to stay behind the men," Lupe says, "but to take our place beside them."

Lupe was born in La Junta, Colorado, on March 12, 1929. Her parents had moved to Colorado from Mexico when her father got a job with the railroad. Each summer the family would go to California to pick fruit. When Lupe was in the fourth grade, the family moved to California.

When Lupe and her sister began school, they could not speak English. Many weeks passed before the girls could understand their teacher or the other students. "That was the worst year of my life," Lupe remembers. However, she would not give up. She continued to work for her education.

Lupe graduated from high school and went to junior college in Ventura, California. When she graduated, she made up her mind to dedicate her life to the church. She entered the convent and began teaching. She loved working with young people. However, she felt a need to help even more people. She said, "I wanted to become involved. I wanted to do more."

Lupe made the difficult decision to leave the convent. She went to work as a counselor for a youth program in East Los Angeles. Soon she was coordinator of a federal poverty program.

Then Lupe went to Washington, D.C., to work for the Department of Health, Education, and Welfare (HEW). There she worked hard to help write the Bilingual Education Act. Once the bill was written, she again worked hard to see that it passed Congress.

Lupe then received a big disappointment. She was not asked to help develop guidelines for the bilingual programs. "I had so many ideas," Lupe remembers, "but after I was left out, I decided to leave HEW."

She had known César Chávez when she was a nun. Chávez's work for *La Causa* appealed to her. She joined the union and became a picket captain in the California vineyards.

César wanted her to go to Michigan to organize a statewide boycott of grapes. Lupe hesitated. She told César that she "just wasn't a leader." César replied, "Do you want to sacrifice the leadership qualities you do have to somebody else?"

Lupe went to Michigan and was very successful. She realized that she *could* be a leader and that there was an important place for a woman in *La Causa*.

She worked for several programs before becoming director of the Southwest Regional Office for the Spanish Speaking at San Antonio, Texas. Her job is an important one. She finds it challenging. "There aren't many Mexican American women who are directors of programs," she says. "It is a difficult job, and many people expect me to follow rather than to lead."

Lupe Anguiano believes strongly that the Mexican American woman has a place in the political affairs of the United States. She spends a great deal of time traveling about the country speaking to Mexican American women. She hopes to make them proud of their heritage and of their sex. "The problems that Chicanas have are similar to the problems most women have," she says, "except that Chicanas are not only women but also minority women."

Lupe helped organize the National Spanish-speaking Women's Caucus. She looks forward to the day when there will be a Spanish-speaking women's center in Washington.

Lupe also helped organize the National Chicana Foundation in Los Angeles.

This organization helps collect writings about Mexican American women. The foundation also helps Mexican American women become more involved in political and cultural activities.

Many times, however, Lupe feels that she is torn between working for the Mexican American people and for women. "Mexican Americans expect me to deal only with ethnic issues," she says. "The women's movement expects me to deal only with women's issues. Yet both ethnic and women's issues are of great importance to me."

Lupe Anguiano Speaking for the United Farm Workers Union in Michigan

Lupe Anguiano is an active woman. She is devoting her life to helping the Mexican American people. She is also working for a better, more active life for all women in the United States. She speaks to all Mexican Americans when she says: "Be proud of your history, your language, and your culture. You will be a better citizen of the United States if you are proud of what you are."

## A. UNDERSTANDING THE STORY

Read each of the following carefully. Then select the correct answer from the choices. Write the letter of the correct answer in the blank that follows each.

1. Lupe Anguiano believes that Mexican American women should (a) not enter politics, (b) take their places beside the men, (c) not work. ............

2. When Lupe first went to school, she had difficulties because she could not (a) speak Spanish, (b) read, (c) speak English. ............

3. Lupe Anguiano left the church because she wanted to (a) teach, (b) become more involved, (c) develop guidelines for bilingual programs. ............

4. When Lupe was asked to go to Michigan, she (a) hesitated at first, (b) immediately accepted, (c) refused to go. ............

5. Lupe's success in Michigan convinced her that (a) she should become a picket captain, (b) women had no place in *La Causa*, (c) she could be a leader. ............

6. Lupe Anguiano hopes Mexican American women will be (a) proud of their heritage, (b) directors of all bilingual programs, (c) less active in politics. ............

7. The National Chicana Foundation helps women become involved in (a) political and cultural activities, (b) political and religious programs, (c) business. ............

8. Sometimes Lupe feels divided when dealing with (a) ethnic and economic issues, (b) political and women's issues, (c) ethnic and women's issues. ............

## B. VOCABULARY

The following words were used in the story. Write a short definition for each word that matches its use in the story. Use a dictionary if necessary.

challenge...................................................................................................

...................................................................................................

minority...................................................................................................

...................................................................................................

disappointment...................................................................................................

...................................................................................................

guideline...................................................................................................

...................................................................................................

appeal..................................................................................................................

..................................................................................................................

ethnic..................................................................................................................

..................................................................................................................

caucus..................................................................................................................

..................................................................................................................

hesitate..................................................................................................................

..................................................................................................................

Sometimes an English word is very similar to its Spanish translation. Fill in each blank with a word from the story that matches the Spanish word.

convento       ...................................................................

sacrificar       ...................................................................

realizar       ...................................................................

comunidad       ...................................................................

dedicar       ...................................................................

## C. THINGS TO TALK ABOUT

Think about the following. Discuss them with your friends or other people you are studying with.

1. What do you think Lupe means when she says Mexican American women should stand beside rather than behind the men? Do you think this also applies to men and women of other ethnic groups?

2. How did Chavéz help Lupe discover her ability to lead? Can you think of other ways to help a person discover his or her talents?

3. Why do some people expect Lupe Anguiano to follow rather than lead, now that she is director of a program?

4. Do you agree with Lupe's statement that people will be better citizens if they are proud of what they are?

8

*Born To Sing*

# Johnny Rodríguez

Johnny Rodríguez grew up in an atmosphere of love and music. He was born in Sabinal, Texas, a small town west of San Antonio. When Johnny was seven years old, his older brother Andy gave him a guitar. Andy could play the guitar and sing very well. Soon his younger brother was doing the same. There were eight children in the family, and they would often gather together to sing.

When Johnny was in junior high school, he organized a musical group called The Spocks, after a television personality, Dr. Spock. "We thought we were really tearing 'em up with our music," Johnny recalls.

However, his school days were not all devoted to playing and singing. He was a star athlete at Sabinal High School. He played basketball and football and participated in track. He also had many part-time jobs—janitor, ranchhand, and ditch digger.

After he graduated, Johnny was not sure what he wanted to do with his life. One thing he did like to do was play his guitar and sing for his food and drink at Garner State Park in the Texas hill country.

One day Johnny and his friends were at this park. "Why don't we have some barbecue?" one of the boys asked.

"We went out and rustled three goats and barbecued them," Johnny recalls. While the group was enjoying their *cabrito*, Texas Ranger Joaquín Jackson drove up. Soon Johnny Rodríguez was in jail on a charge of goat rustling. While Johnny was in jail, he amused himself by playing his guitar and singing.

Ranger Jackson heard the young man singing in his cell and took him to meet James T. "Happy" Shahan. Shahan was the operator of Alamo Village Vacationland, a tourist attraction near Bracketville, Texas. When the judge gave Johnny a probated sentence, Shahan gave him a job.

Johnny acted in skits and worked at the Shahan ranch. Shahan helped Johnny with his singing. "Now," says Shahan, "some people say he sounds just like Merle Haggard, but he's strictly Johnny Rodríguez."

Today Happy Shahan still helps manage Johnny's career. Ranger Jackson also remains one of Johnny Rodríguez's good friends and loyal fans. "Johnny's really a great young man, just a typical young American," Jackson says.

Johnny got his first big opportunity when recording star Tom T. Hall came to Bracketville to hear Johnny sing. A year later Johnny went to Nashville to join Hall's band. Tom suggested that Johnny have his hair cut and styled. Shahan added some western-style clothes and a pair of cowboy boots. However, there was one thing Johnny would not do. "I won't wear sequins," he said.

The people at Mercury Records didn't need to see sequins to know that Johnny Rodríguez would be a hit in the country-western field. All they had to do was listen to him play and sing "I Can't Stop Loving You," both in Spanish and in English. They signed him to a contract, and soon the first "Johnny Rod" hit, "Pass Me By," was the number one song in Nashville.

Johnny's next three single records also became number one on the record charts. His first two albums "Introducing Johnny Rodríguez" and "All I Ever Meant To Do Was Sing" soon became hits. Johnny Rodríguez had become a famous recording star.

On February 26, 1973, Johnny Rodríguez won a Grammy Award from the Academy of Country-Western Music as

the "Most Promising Vocalist, 1972." In March 1973 Rodríguez appeared at the famous auditorium, Carnegie Hall.

One day Johnny went back to Texas to visit a place where he used to play his guitar and sing. He said, "I went back and everybody looked like they'd seen a ghost. They said, 'We never thought you'd come back over here.' It kind of made me feel bad in a way, because people tend to think that you forget. But after about half an hour, it was just like the good old days."

Tom T. Hall says that for Johnny Rodríguez the best of his good old days are still to come.

## A. UNDERSTANDING THE STORY

Read each of the following carefully. Then select the correct answer from the choices. Write the letter of the correct answer in the blank that follows each.

1. Johnny Rodríguez learned to play the guitar (a) by himself, (b) from his brother, (c) from Happy Shahan. ............

2. During high school, Johnny devoted his time to singing and to (a) working at Happy Shahan's ranch, (b) recording, (c) sports.  ............

3. Johnny was arrested for (a) goat rustling, (b) cattle rustling, (c) disturbing the peace.  ............

4. Johnny Rodríguez left the Shahan ranch to (a) join Merle Haggard's band, (b) work at Garner State Park, (c) join Tom T. Hall's band.  ............

5. The people at Mercury Records (a) hesitated to sign Johnny to a contract, (b) felt Johnny would be a hit, (c) asked Johnny to wear sequins.  ............

6. The first four recordings of Johnny Rodríguez (a) were failures, (b) reached number one on the record charts, (c) were slightly successful.  ............

7. The Academy of Country-Western Music named Johnny the (a) "Most Promising Vocalist" of the year, (b) "Best Vocalist" of the year, (c) "Best Guitar Player" of the year.  ............

8. When Johnny returned to Texas, his friends at first (a) were surprised to see him, (b) were angry at him, (c) ignored him completely.  ............

## B. VOCABULARY

A synonym is a word having the same or almost the same meaning as another word. Match these words with their synonyms by writing them in the blanks.

atmosphere    tourist    sentence
gather    opportunity    amuse
rustle    style    auditorium

1. traveler  .................................................

2. fashion  .................................................

3. surroundings  .................................................

4. entertain  .................................................

5. hall  .................................................

6. chance  .................................................

7. assemble  .................................................

8. steal  .................................................

9. judgment  .................................................

## C. THINGS TO WRITE ABOUT

Answer the following questions on the lines provided.

1. After graduating from high school, Johnny Rodríguez was not sure what he wanted to do in life. Why do you think many young people sometimes feel this way?

..........................................................................................................................................

..........................................................................................................................................

..........................................................................................................................................

..........................................................................................................................................

..........................................................................................................................................

..........................................................................................................................................

2. Why were Johnny Rodríguez's friends surprised when Johnny returned to a place in Texas where he used to play and sing?

..........................................................................................................................................

..........................................................................................................................................

..........................................................................................................................................

..........................................................................................................................................

..........................................................................................................................................

..........................................................................................................................................

3. At first Johnny felt bad about his friends' reaction when he returned to Texas. What does this tell you about the character of Johnny Rodríguez?

..........................................................................................................................................

..........................................................................................................................................

..........................................................................................................................................

..........................................................................................................................................

..........................................................................................................................................

..........................................................................................................................................

# Julián Nava

Photographic Office, Los Angeles City School Districts

"When I was growing up," says Julián Nava, "I thought that Anglos were smarter than Mexicans." He remembers that his school counselors advised him to become an auto mechanic. However, Julián dreamed of being a teacher. He knew he could be one if he really tried. He also dreamed of entering politics one day.

Politics had shaped the fortunes of the Nava family even before Julián was born. His parents came to the United States to escape the revolution in Mexico. First they went to Texas and then to California. Julián was born in 1927 in the Boyle Heights area of East Los Angeles.

When young Julián was old enough, he often went to his father's barbershop. He listened to the people talking about politics. He also watched his father string guitars and carve chess pieces by hand. Both his love of politics and his love of the arts developed in his father's barbershop.

When Julián graduated from high school, he joined the navy. There he dis-covered many people who did not care if a person was an Anglo, a Mexican American, or a black. In the navy it was the job that counted. This inspired Julián. He decided to go to school to study history.

When the war was over, Julián entered East Los Angeles Junior College. He was an A student and was elected president of the student body. Then he went on to earn a degree from Pomona College. Good grades helped him win grants to Harvard University. There he completed his doctor's degree.

Dr. Julián Nava returned to California to teach history at San Fernando Valley State College, now California State University at Northridge. One of the many things he wanted to do was to write the story of the Mexican Americans. "The history of the Mexican American has yet to be written," he says.

Dr. Nava's book, *Mexican Americans: Past, Present, and Future*, helps to tell this story. It is written in both Spanish and English. Dr. Nava has also written a bilingual reading series that is used by many children in the public schools. Some of his other books are *The Mexican American in American History* and *Viva La Raza: Readings on Mexican Americans.*

Dr. Nava has written these books because he hopes that the old myths about his people will be replaced by the true story of their history. "Most history is the account of winners," he says. "Mexican Americans are identified as losers in almost all works of history that deal with them." His books try to give new facts and data about Mexican Americans. He shows them as true achievers and contributors to American culture.

Although he was a success as a teacher and as an author of textbooks, Dr. Nava still remembered his love of politics. From his early days in his father's barbershop until his teaching days in California, he had wanted to enter politics. In 1967 he decided to run for a place on the Los Angeles Board of Education.

He was the first Mexican American in this century to run for this office. Dr. Nava campaigned throughout the city. The people who helped him in the race came from all parts of Los Angeles. Ju-

Breaking Ground for a New Cafeteria at an Elementary School in Los Angeles

lián wanted to serve not only the Mexican Americans but all the people. When he won, he knew that he had won because people from all groups had voted for him—not just Mexican Americans.

Later, Dr. Nava became president of the board. When his term was about to end, he decided to run again. Six other candidates ran against him. He won with 51 percent of the vote. Once again he pledged to represent all the people.

Dr. Nava's career has been devoted to showing the contributions of Mexican Americans to American life. He also has tried to break down prejudice. However, he realizes that some prejudice comes from Mexican Americans also. "Racism and prejudice are found among minorities as well as among the majority," he says. "When Mexican American youths call an Anglo American a 'gabacho,' it is the same as an Anglo calling a Mexican American a 'greaser.'"

Julián Nava Serving on the Los Angeles Board of Education

Dr. Julián Nava believes that Mexican American history is "more than just past politics." His books often deal with the lives of ordinary people. He is one historian who will not let his people be forgotten or ignored.

## A. UNDERSTANDING THE STORY

Read each of the following carefully. Then select the correct answer from the choices. Write the letter of the correct answer in the blank that follows each.

1. When Julián was young, he thought that (a) Mexican Americans were smarter than Anglos, (b) Anglos were smarter than Mexican Americans, (c) he would like to be an auto mechanic. ............

2. Julián's parents came to the United States to escape (a) the migrant stream, (b) the revolution, (c) a poor climate. ............

3. In his father's barbershop, Julián developed a love of (a) chess, (b) guitars, (c) politics and art. ............

4. In the navy, Julián learned that many people didn't (a) like him, (b) mind that he was a Mexican American, (c) care how he performed his duties. ............

5. When Julián returned to California, he decided to (a) teach math, (b) complete his law degree, (c) study history. ............

6. Dr. Nava's books tell the story of the Mexican American's (a) history, (b) music, (c) politics. ............

7. Nava hopes his writings will help replace old myths with (a) political information, (b) newer myths, (c) true history. ............

8. Julián Nava has devoted his career to showing (a) the contributions of Mexican Americans to American life, (b) the prejudices found among people, (c) that Mexican American history is mostly past politics. ............

9. According to Dr. Nava, there is a need to eliminate prejudice among Anglos as well as among (a) Mexican Americans, (b) the majority group, (c) historians. ............

10. Nava's books (a) are about important people only, (b) often deal with the lives of ordinary people, (c) may someday be forgotten. ............

# B. VOCABULARY

Match each word in Column A with its meaning in Column B by writing the letter of the meaning in the blank in front of the word.

| Column A | Column B |
|----------|----------|
| ............ 1. term | a. to take the place of |
| ............ 2. contributor | b. ideas, skills, arts, tools, and way of life of a people |
| ............ 3. myth | c. dislike of people because of their race |
| ............ 4. achiever | d. to work to get elected |
| ............ 5. replace | e. time a person holds a position |
| ............ 6. campaign | f. false idea about something |
| ............ 7. grant | g. a person who gives |
| ............ 8. culture | h. a person who does things |
| ............ 9. data | i. money given to help a person in some task |
| ............ 10. prejudice | j. information |

# C. THINGS TO TALK ABOUT

Think about the following. Discuss them with your friends or other people you are studying with.

1. Dr. Nava says that when he was young he thought Anglos were smarter than Mexican Americans. How can this kind of thinking affect a person?

2. In the navy, Dr. Nava found that people didn't care what race he belonged to, but they did care about how he did his job. Which do you think is more important, and why do you think so?

3. Dr. Nava feels that Mexican Americans are true contributors to American culture. Can you think of some of these contributions? If possible, obtain some of Dr. Nava's books to help you find some contributions.

# Henry B. González

Henry B. González has been a fighter all his life. When he decided to run for an elected office, he asked various political leaders for help. "A Mexican cannot win," they told him. In spite of this, Henry decided to try. He ran for the Texas legislature. His was the only Mexican American name on the ballot. He lost the race. Instead of being discouraged, however, he was determined to try again and win.

Henry B. González has always had to struggle. When he first went to school in San Antonio, Texas, he could not speak English. There were only a few Mexican American children in class; the rest were Anglos. Henry was afraid and would not speak to anyone.

One day a second-grade teacher entered his room. She spoke both Spanish and English. She told young Henry that she knew he could be one of the best students in class, and she looked forward to teaching him next year. Her words were all Henry needed. Soon he was learning to read and write English.

While he was still in grade school,

Henry began to work. At work, he first experienced discrimination. He was often called "greaser" and not allowed to enter places marked "for whites only."

Henry was also confused about his identity. "I was in the second grade before I realized I wasn't a Mexican," he remembers. "A teacher looked at my records and said, 'You're an American.' After that I wondered: What am I?"

After much thinking, Henry convinced himself that he didn't have to be confused or ashamed. "This is my land," he said. "I'm part of it. Why should I be an alien? I was born here."

After graduating from high school, Henry went to San Antonio Junior College. He transferred to The University of Texas to study engineering. However, during the Great Depression, he had to quit school to go to work.

Still Henry refused to give up. Several years later, he returned to college at St. Mary's University in San Antonio. There he earned a law degree.

Instead of practicing law, however, Henry decided to work helping the

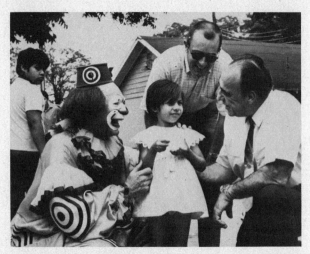

González often attends parties and fiestas to keep in touch with members of his district.

young people of San Antonio. He became a juvenile probation officer. He left this job when World War II broke out, but he returned to serve as chief probation officer. He quit that position when a judge refused to let him hire a black on an equal basis with the rest of the staff.

In 1950 Henry B. González ran for the state legislature and lost. He decided that if he could not be in state government, he would participate in city government. He ran for a place on the city council of San Antonio. This time he won the election.

Then, in 1956, after a hard campaign, he became the first senator of Mexican descent in the Texas legislature in over one hundred years. He stayed there five years. Again, he proved he was a fighter. He became famous for a thirty-six hour filibuster which helped defeat eight "race bills." These bills were meant to uphold the principle of segregation.

In 1961 there was a special election for a vacant seat in the U.S. House of Representatives. Henry B. González entered the race and won. He has served in the U.S. Congress ever since.

There he has worked hard for many causes, such as fair housing, benefits for farm workers, equal education, a minimum wage, and equal opportunity for all people—regardless of race, creed, or sex. He says, "I support programs which help those who need it most."

Henry B. González was very active in the election campaigns of Presidents Kennedy and Johnson. He also helped Humphrey and McGovern in their presidential campaigns.

Henry also worked hard for many years to help bring to San Antonio a world's fair (HemisFair). The city benefited greatly from the attention and commerce HemisFair brought.

Congressman González has written many articles for magazines and has also given many speeches. Despite this busy schedule, however, he finds time to spend with his wife, their eight children, and their grandchildren.

In one of his speeches Henry B. González said, "If my political career was aimed at proving any one point, that point is that the fact I am a person of Mexican descent does not mean I cannot attain political goals." Henry B. González has indeed attained many goals, and he continues to fight for the things he believes in.

Speaking to Students at a School in San Antonio

# A. UNDERSTANDING THE STORY

Read each of the following carefully. Then select the correct answer from the choices. Write the letter of the correct answer in the blank that follows each.

1. When Henry B. González first ran for public office, other political leaders (a) offered to help him, (b) told him he would win easily, (c) told him a Mexican couldn't win. ............

2. At first Henry had difficulties in school until (a) he learned to read, (b) a teacher encouraged him to learn, (c) he began to work. ............

3. When Henry was young, he was confused about (a) discrimination, (b) learning English, (c) his identity. ............

4. During the Great Depression, Henry had to (a) transfer to another college, (b) quit work, (c) quit school. ............

5. Henry B. González was the first person of Mexican descent in over a hundred years elected to the (a) city council of San Antonio, (b) Texas senate, (c) U.S. House of Representatives. ............

6. Since 1961 Henry B. González has served in the U.S. (a) House of Representatives (b) Senate, (c) Office of Equal Opportunity. ............

7. Congressman González has worked for many causes such as (a) segregation, (b) equal education and a minimum wage, (c) fewer benefits for farm workers. ............

8. Henry B. González says his political career was aimed at proving that Mexican Americans (a) can attain political goals, (b) shouldn't run for office, (c) should not fight discrimination. ............

# B. VOCABULARY

The following words were used in the story. Write a short definition for each word that matches its use in the story. Use a dictionary if necessary.

ballot ..................................................................................................

..................................................................................................

discrimination ..................................................................................................

..................................................................................................

identity ..................................................................................................

..................................................................................................

filibuster ..................................................................................................

..................................................................................................

segregation ................................................................................................................

................................................................................................................

commerce ................................................................................................................

................................................................................................................

schedule ................................................................................................................

................................................................................................................

uphold ................................................................................................................

................................................................................................................

## C. THINGS TO WRITE ABOUT

Answer the following questions on the lines provided.

1. Why was Henry confused about his identity? What can be done to help bi-cultural children with the same problem?

................................................................................................................

................................................................................................................

................................................................................................................

................................................................................................................

................................................................................................................

................................................................................................................

................................................................................................................

2. What do you think is the most important thing Henry B. González has done? Why do you think so?

................................................................................................................

................................................................................................................

................................................................................................................

................................................................................................................

................................................................................................................

................................................................................................................

................................................................................................................

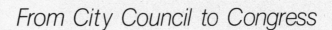

# Edward R. Roybal

Edward R. Roybal is a person with strong opinions. "I feel that education provides the main answer to the problems of Mexican Americans," he says. "Equal educational opportunities have been denied to Mexican Americans in the past."

Edward R. Roybal is a member of the United States House of Representatives. He helped write the Bilingual Education Act. Roybal constantly fights for more and better opportunities in employment and education for Spanish-speaking people.

Edward was born in Albuquerque, New Mexico, on February 10, 1916. His family moved to the Boyle Heights *barrio* of Los Angeles when he was four years old.

When Edward was in school, he considered withdrawing in order to work to help his family. "My mother insisted that I stay in school," Roybal remembers, "and a junior high school teacher inspired me to get as much education as I could."

Roybal graduated from Roosevelt High School. "The day I graduated from high school was the happiest day of my life," he recalls. "I was the first in my family for several generations to make it all the way through high school."

Roybal wanted to continue his education, but the country was then in the Great Depression. Times were hard everywhere. College was often a luxury reserved for wealthy people only.

Roybal joined the Civilian Conservation Corps. This was a federal program in which young people who could not find jobs worked on public projects.

Edward managed to save much of the twenty-five dollars he made each month working for the CCC. He also saved the money he earned working in a dry cleaning plant.

Soon he had enough money to go to college. He studied business administration at UCLA and then went to law school at Southwestern University.

Roybal had always been interested in health, and in 1941 he became a public health administrator for the California Tuberculosis Association. His work took

West Los Angeles Community Service Organization

Voter registration campaigns helped Roybal to be elected to the Los Angeles City Council.

Roybal and his friends also organized a voter registration drive in the *barrios.* They showed the people how to vote to elect officials who would help them.

When Roybal ran for the city council a second time, voters from the *barrios* helped him win. Roybal worked hard on the city council. He was particularly concerned with public health and welfare.

In 1962 Roybal decided that he could help the people even more by serving in the U.S. House of Representatives. He ran for a seat from a newly formed district and won the race.

Roybal has had many duties in Congress. However, he has always found time to help write bills to help Mexican Americans.

One of the most important of these bills was the Bilingual Education Act. This law helps schools set up bilingual programs for Mexican American children. The programs help children whose home language is not English.

Roybal has also helped pass bills to give benefits to veterans, senior citizens, and migrant workers. He has also spoken out for better health programs and for environmental education.

Edward Roybal has dedicated his life to serving people, especially Mexican Americans. "I am constantly fighting government officials," he says, "urging them to extend equal opportunities to Mexican Americans." He feels that Mexican Americans in this country should "obtain a full share of the great economic, social, and educational benefits of this land."

him into the *barrios* of Los Angeles. He saw poverty, poor health, little education, and few opportunities.

The young public health worker decided to do something about these conditions. He thought the best way he could help Mexican Americans was to run for a seat on the Los Angeles City Council. He ran for the office but lost. However, he received four thousand votes—more than any other Mexican American had ever received in Los Angeles.

Roybal and a group of his former campaign workers decided to form the Community Service Organization. Together they fought against discrimination in housing, employment, and education.

## A. UNDERSTANDING THE STORY

Read each of the following carefully. Then select the correct answer from the choices. Write the letter of the correct answer in the blank that follows each.

1. Edward Roybal believes that the main solution to the problems of Mexican Americans is (a) employment, (b) education, (c) equal rights.

............

2. Roybal was encouraged to stay in school by his (a) mother and a grade school teacher, (b) father and a junior high school teacher, (c) mother and a junior high school teacher. ............

3. Roybal says the happiest day of his life was when he (a) graduated from high school, (b) was elected to Congress, (c) joined the CCC. ............

4. The Great Depression made obtaining a college education difficult for (a) wealthy people, (b) most people except the wealthy, (c) all people. ............

5. When Roybal saw the poor living conditions of people in the *barrios* of Los Angeles, he (a) decided to become a public health administrator, (b) joined the CCC, (c) decided to run for the city council. ............

6. Roybal won a seat on the city council with help from (a) farm workers, (b) voters from the *barrios*, (c) members of the Civilian Conservation Corps. ............

7. Bilingual programs help children (a) who cannot speak Spanish, (b) whose home language is English, (c) whose home language is not English. ............

8. Edward Roybal hopes Mexican Americans will receive (a) equal opportunities, (b) fewer benefits, (c) more land. ............

## B. VOCABULARY

A synonym is a word having the same or almost the same meaning as another word. Match these words with their synonyms by writing them in the blanks.

| denied | inspire | share |
|--------|---------|-------|
| provide | condition | set |
| wealthy | benefits | |

1. advantages ...............................................................

2. refused ...............................................................

3. establish ...............................................................

4. give ...............................................................

5. situation ...............................................................

6. rich ...............................................................

7. portion ...............................................................

8. affect ...............................................................

## C. THINGS TO WRITE ABOUT

Answer the following questions on the lines provided.

1. Give some examples that show Roybal's strong feelings about education.

.......................................................................................................
.......................................................................................................
.......................................................................................................
.......................................................................................................
.......................................................................................................
.......................................................................................................
.......................................................................................................

2. What helped Roybal to be elected the second time he ran for the city council?

.......................................................................................................
.......................................................................................................
.......................................................................................................
.......................................................................................................
.......................................................................................................
.......................................................................................................
.......................................................................................................

3. What is bilingual education? Do you think having such programs is a good idea?

.......................................................................................................
.......................................................................................................
.......................................................................................................
.......................................................................................................
.......................................................................................................
.......................................................................................................

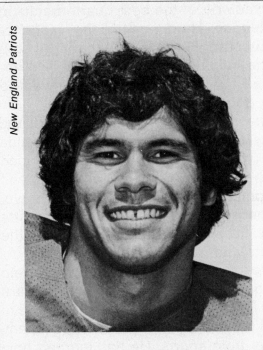

New England Patriots

*First String Quarterback*

# Jim Plunkett

Being "number one" has become a way of life for Jim Plunkett. When he played football for Stanford University in California, he was the All-American choice of seven voting groups. Jim also won the 1970 Heisman Trophy, one of the greatest honors a college football player can receive. He was the number one draft choice of the National Football League the following year.

However, being number one is not always easy. Jack Schultz, a captain of his college football team, recalls, "Jim wasn't born All-American. He had to struggle for everything he ever had or did, on or off the field. He's the hardest worker on the team."

Jim Plunkett learned hard work from his family. His mother was blind, and his father had poor sight. They lived in San Jose, California. His father worked in a restaurant and also ran a newsstand.

"I got a lot of support from both my parents," Jim recalls. "It wasn't until later, looking back, that I found anything unusual in having blind parents."

Jim began playing football in the fifth grade. When he was in the eighth grade, he started playing quarterback. "I found out I could throw," he says. Jim led his team to the county championship.

Jim also worked during his school years. He mowed lawns, gardened, and had a newspaper route.

In high school, Jim had knee trouble. His knees were taped for each game. At first he played poorly, but slowly he improved. In his last two years, Jim was named to the All-League team.

After graduation Jim entered Stanford University. However, a thyroid tumor that required surgery was discovered in the left side of his neck. Because of this, Jim was late for freshman football. He missed the opening game and played badly in the games he did play.

Stanford had good quarterbacks, so Jim did not play his second year. He spent the season "warming the bench."

However, with the first game of the 1968 season Jim Plunkett was the starting quarterback. He played extremely well. By the end of the season, he had passed for more yardage than any other player in the history of his conference.

The next season Jim again set many passing records. At the end of this season, he was eligible to play professional football. However, since Jim had not played during his second year, he could also choose to play one more year for Stanford.

Jim chose to remain in school. He told his coach, "If I were to leave now, I would always have the feeling that I let the team down. Besides, we are always telling kids today not to drop out, to finish school, to set targets, and to work toward them. What would they think if I were to drop out now for professional football?"

Jim's decision was wise. His next year brought even more achievements. His team won the conference. Then, in the Rose Bowl, Stanford defeated powerful and unbeaten Ohio State. One of the coaches for a rival team called Plunkett "the best college football player I've ever seen."

A few months after the Rose Bowl game, Jim signed a contract with the New England Patriots. He found playing professional football different from the college game. "I didn't know what to expect starting professional football," he says. "I didn't know what things I could do or what things I could accomplish as a rookie. But at times I felt I was doing a good job. But there were other times I didn't feel I was throwing the ball as well as I could have." At the end of the season, he was named "Rookie of the Year."

Many people think Jim Plunkett can become one of the best quarterbacks in the league. Hard work is the secret of his success. He says, "Every time I step on the field, I've got to say that I've improved from the previous time. I want to be a good quarterback."

Like many other Mexican Americans in the sports field, Jim Plunkett spends time working with Mexican American boys and girls. He tries to get athletic equipment for groups of young people. He believes that taking part in sports helps keep many young people off the streets and out of trouble.

Jim says, "I think that sports can help and does help all kids. I think they learn a lot of good lessons from them." Jim Plunkett certainly has learned many things from sports. He has learned how to make himself a "winner."

# A. UNDERSTANDING THE STORY

Read each of the following carefully. Then select the correct answer from the choices. Write the letter of the correct answer in the blank that follows each.

1. The only honor Jim Plunkett didn't receive was (a) All-American, (b) the Heisman Trophy, (c) Most Valuable Player. ............

2. Jack Schultz feels that Jim (a) didn't deserve to become an All-American, (b) was born an All-American, (c) had to struggle for everything.  ............

3. Jim Plunkett learned about hard work from (a) the captain of his football team, (b) his family, (c) his football coach.  ............

4. In the eighth grade, Jim discovered he (a) had a thyroid tumor, (b) could throw well, (c) had knee trouble.  ............

5. Jim chose to remain at Stanford one more year because (a) he could earn more money, (b) he wished to help the team and to set a good example, (c) his coach convinced him to stay.  ............

6. Jim signed his first professional football contract with (a) Stanford, (b) the New England Patriots, (c) the Los Angeles Rams.  ............

7. Many people think Jim Plunkett can become one of the (a) worst players in the league, (b) best running backs in the league, (c) best quarterbacks in the league.  ............

8. Jim Plunkett believes that sports help keep young people (a) off the streets, (b) in trouble, (c) in touch with life.  ............

## B. VOCABULARY

Match each word in Column A with its meaning in Column B by writing the letter of the meaning in the blank in front of the word.

| | **Column A** | | **Column B** |
|---|---|---|---|
| ............ | 1. achievement | a. | to work hard for |
| ............ | 2. eligible | b. | needed |
| ............ | 3. rival | c. | very much |
| ............ | 4. struggle | d. | something to work for, goal |
| ............ | 5. unbeaten | e. | a thing done or something gained |
| .......... | 6. required | f. | engaged in an activity for pay |
| .......... | 7. extremely | g. | fit to be chosen |
| ............ | 8. target | h. | not defeated |
| ............ | 9. support | i. | person or group trying to get the same thing as another |
| ............ | 10. professional | j. | help |

## C. THINGS TO WRITE ABOUT

Answer the following questions on the lines provided.

1. What does being "number one" mean to Jim Plunkett? What does it mean to you?

......................................................................................................................

......................................................................................................................

......................................................................................................................

......................................................................................................................

......................................................................................................................

......................................................................................................................

......................................................................................................................

2. What do you think of Jim's reasons for remaining in college an extra year?

......................................................................................................................

......................................................................................................................

......................................................................................................................

......................................................................................................................

......................................................................................................................

......................................................................................................................

......................................................................................................................

3. Jim says sports help young people learn many good lessons. What things can a young person learn from sports?

......................................................................................................................

......................................................................................................................

......................................................................................................................

......................................................................................................................

......................................................................................................................

......................................................................................................................

Marion Koogler McNay Art Institute

# Consuelo "Chelo" Amezcua

"I love nature, shaded trees, singing birds, the soft breeze, blooming bushes, butterflies, sweet perfume, and light blue skies. I have a world in my mind full of joy and full of art." These are the words of Consuelo Amezcua, who signs her paintings and poems with the name "Chelo."

Chelo was born in Piedras Negras, Mexico, in 1903. When she was a child, her family moved to Del Rio, Texas. Her parents were both teachers. They had two daughters, Chelo and her sister Zare, and four sons.

Chelo says of her parents, "They always tried to create happiness for us. They played the guitar and sang with joy. This family of mine took care of me. I was something special to them."

The artist still lives in Del Rio, although her paintings have been shown in many places. Her life has been a happy one. Chelo says, "I keep childhood in my heart even though I am over seventy years old."

Chelo began drawing when she was just five years old. She used to draw on the walls of her home. Chelo says that her parents "always kept me with a wet rag cleaning the walls where I wanted to express my inspirations." Later, Chelo

Marion Koogler McNay Art Institute

*Texas Hurraca* by Chelo

29

would draw with a pencil on scraps of paper or on cardboard.

Chelo wanted to go to Mexico to study to be a painter. She wrote a letter to President Cárdenas of Mexico asking for a scholarship to go to the Academy of San Carlos. The scholarship was granted, but before the young girl could make the trip, her father died. She decided to stay with her mother and go to work.

However, she never lost her desire to paint. She spent long hours drawing and coloring. She also began to write poetry. One of her poems reads:

> What's in your soul
> Sooner or later
> Reveals when
> You are a good
> Servant of the Lord.
> If you have been
> Faithful to the Master
> Seek your
> Inner-self
> And you will
> Find knowledge.

Often Chelo went to the banks of the Pecos River. She took her chisel and carved figures on the smooth surfaces of the rocks that lay on the ground. Chelo would say, "I'll caress you with my chisel to transform you into a Jewel Box." She often sang as she carved.

Most artists paint on canvas with brushes, but not Chelo. She draws on cardboard or paper and uses ball-point pens of many different colors. First she sketches in the outlines of the forms and figures. Then she fills in the details. She must take pains to be sure that each line is exactly right. Many times she includes a poem in her paintings. In her work, "Hands of Texans," there is a poem that reads:

> Hands fly and trace lines as
> Thoughts command

And never finish for Art has No end.

Chelo calls her work, "Filigree Art." Because her paintings are made of many lines, they look like lacy spider webs.

There are many figures in Chelo's paintings. Sometimes there are birds and animals. Many times there are famous persons. She has also done many paintings of hands.

Chelo gets many of the subjects for her paintings from Mexican culture. One of her paintings is called "El Magnífico Poeta." It is a painting of Nezahualcóyotl, the Indian ruler who was a patron of the arts. His palace in Texcoco was rich and splendid. Another of her paintings is titled "Moctezuma, King of Mexico." She also has one called "Mexico Americans."

Marion Koogler McNay Art Institute

The Artist's *Sevillana*

Chelo's paintings have been shown in many cities. She has also won awards for her poetry. Many people recognize Chelo as one of the Southwest's great Mexican American artists.

Chelo keeps her childhood through her paintings and poetry. She has found happiness in her life and speaks of it in one of her poems:

Happiness is a treasure
Given to us by our Lord
Is a truth in our lives
Is a feeling in our souls
That satisfies.

## A. UNDERSTANDING THE STORY

Read each of the following carefully. Then select the correct answer from the choices. Write the letter of the correct answer in the blank that follows each.

1. Chelo says her parents (a) lived in a world of joy and art, (b) kept their childhoods in their hearts, (c) considered her someone special. ............

2. Chelo began drawing (a) when she was over seventy years old, (b) at the Academy of San Carlos, (c) when she was five. ............

3. A scholarship was granted to Chelo to attend the Academy of San Carlos, but she (a) lost her desire to paint, (b) didn't go because of the death of her father, (c) decided she didn't need to study art. ............

4. Most artists paint on canvas with brushes, but Chelo paints on (a) the smooth surfaces of rocks, (b) cardboard with pencils, (c) cardboard with ball-point pens. ............

5. Chelo calls her work (a) "Filigree Art," (b) "Hands of Texans," (c) "Lacy Spiderweb Art." ............

6. Many of the subjects for Chelo's paintings come from (a) Mexican culture, (b) the Southwest, (c) Del Rio, Texas. ............

7. Nezahualcóyotl was (a) the name of a palace in Texcoco, (b) the king of Mexico, (c) an Indian ruler who was a patron of the arts. ............

8. Many people consider Chelo one of the (a) greatest artists of all time, (b) Southwest's great Mexican American artists, (c) greatest poets in America. ............

9. Chelo says she (a) remains young through her art, (b) is unhappy, (c) keeps her childhood through her friends. ............

## B. VOCABULARY

An antonym is a word which has the opposite meaning of another word. Match these words with their antonyms by writing them in the blanks.

joy           includes        famous
create      smooth        splendid
granted     express

1. awful     ...........................................................

2. rough     ...........................................................

3. excludes     ...........................................................

4. unknown     ...........................................................

5. destroy     ...........................................................

6. repress     ...........................................................

7. sadness     ...........................................................

8. denied     ...........................................................

## C. THINGS TO TALK ABOUT

Think about the following. Discuss them with your friends or other people you are studying with.

1. What does Chelo mean when she says, "I keep childhood in my heart"?

2. What do you think about Chelo's poems? What do they tell you about her as a person?

Photo by John Ebling

# José Ángel Gutiérrez

José Ángel Gutiérrez is very much a part of a new political movement. He is one of the many reasons why many Mexican Americans cry, "¡Viva La Raza!" with a growing sense of pride.

In 1970 José Ángel established a new political party, La Raza Unida. His dream is to make it an important influence in politics wherever Mexican Americans live in the United States.

José Ángel was born on October 25, 1944, in the town of Crystal City, Texas. His father, a doctor, fought in Mexico with Francisco "Pancho" Villa in the Mexican revolution. As a result of the turmoil, the elder Gutiérrez was forced into exile and came to Crystal City.

When José Ángel was young, his parents enrolled him with other Mexican American children in the Little School of 400. It was so named because the teachers taught the children 400 basic words so that they could do well in school. "It's the only way you could survive," says Gutiérrez.

Since he had light skin and his father was a doctor, José Ángel was accepted by Anglo members of the community. However, when José Ángel was twelve, his father died. Soon the family's savings were gone. People no longer treated him and his family with so much respect. Many merchants denied the family credit, and José Ángel's mother was forced to work in the fields to earn a living.

Gutiérrez began to notice what he considered unfair treatment of Chicanos in the schools, as well as in the community. He saw that they seldom held important positions or received important honors. One incident that José Ángel particularly remembers was when the principal of his high school rejected the outcome of a student election because, as José Ángel put it, "Too many Chicanos had won positions."

José Ángel received his first taste of politics in high school. He was elected president of the student body. He also worked for PASO, the Political Association of Spanish-speaking Organizations.

PASO helped elect five Mexican Americans to the city council of Crystal

José Ángel talks with a group of students at St. Mary's University in San Antonio.

City. These elected officials, however, lacked political knowledge and experience, and the effort was considered by many to be a failure.

After graduation José Ángel went to Texas A&I University where he studied political science. Later, he went to St. Mary's University in San Antonio to study for his master's degree. While he was at St. Mary's, he helped organize MAYO, the Mexican American Youth Organization.

Some people considered MAYO too militant. Others claimed that MAYO's militancy was never more than words. "We haven't burned down anything," one MAYO leader said, "and we don't intend to."

When José Ángel organized La Raza Unida, the party held its first campaign in Crystal City. Gutiérrez's political knowledge and experience proved to be very useful. The party gained control of the city's school board. José Ángel was one of those elected to the board. He later became president of the board.

Many changes began to occur in the school system. Bilingual education was introduced in the schools. Many Mexican American teachers and teachers'

aides were hired. The school district's budget was increased from one million to three million dollars.

By 1973 La Raza Unida not only controlled the school board but the city government of Crystal City as well. Again many new programs to help Mexican Americans were started. Chicanos began to fill important positions in government as well as business. The Mexican Americans of the city no longer felt powerless. They knew they now had a voice in their government.

The success of the party surprised even Gutiérrez. When the party held a convention in El Paso, Texas, nearly 2,500 people attended. "Now Chicanos all over Texas want to pull a Crystal City of their own," Gutiérrez said.

Many Anglos and some Chicanos believe that Gutiérrez is too militant and revolutionary. However, Gutiérrez feels that he is fighting for justice in the way he knows best, through politics.

Campaigning for County Judge

José Ángel continues his struggle for justice by serving as county judge of Zavala County in Crystal City. He says, "For too long justice was only for Anglos. Today we are opening wider the doors of opportunity our ancestors kicked, knocked, and scratched on."

For many people, Crystal City and La Raza Unida have become symbols of what organized Mexican Americans can accomplish. Many now say, *"Sí se puede"*—"It can be done."

## A. UNDERSTANDING THE STORY

Read each of the following carefully. Then select the correct answer from the choices. Write the letter of the correct answer in the blank that follows each.

1. José Ángel's father fought in (a) the American Civil War, (b) Mexico against Pancho Villa, (c) the Mexican revolution with Pancho Villa. ............

2. When José Ángel was young, he attended (a) the School of 300, (b) PASO, (c) the Little School of 400. ............

3. After his father's death, José Ángel and his family were (a) treated with respect, (b) given extra credit, (c) treated with less respect than before. ............

4. José Ángel received his first taste of politics (a) in high school, (b) at St. Mary's University, (c) in junior high school. ............

5. Some people thought that the members of MAYO (a) were too political, (b) were too militant, (c) lacked political knowledge and experience. ............

6. José Ángel was first elected, (a) to the city council of Crystal City, (b) to the school board of Crystal City, (c) mayor of Crystal City. ............

7. After La Raza Unida gained control of the school board, (a) the school district's budget was increased from one million to two million dollars, (b) few changes occurred, (c) bilingual education was introduced in the schools. ............

8. As La Raza Unida expanded, the Mexican Americans of Crystal City began to (a) feel powerless, (b) hold conventions in their city, (c) feel they had a voice in their government. ............

## B. VOCABULARY

Match each word in Column A with its meaning in Column B by writing the letter of the meaning in the blank in front of the word.

| | Column A | | Column B |
|---|---|---|---|
| ............ | 1. exile | a. | to complete something |
| ............ | 2. influence | b. | amount of money available to an organization |
| ............ | 3. merchant | c. | to not have something |
| ............ | 4. rejected | d. | expulsion from home |
| ............ | 5. budget | e. | behavior towards another |
| ............ | 6. knowledge | f. | person or thing that has the power to affect others |
| ............ | 7. lack | g. | refused to accept |
| ............ | 8. treatment | h. | information a person has learned |
| ............ | 9. accomplish | i. | disturbance |
| ............ | 10. turmoil | j. | storekeeper |

Sometimes an English word is very similar to its Spanish translation. Fill in each blank with a word from the story that matches the Spanish word.

influencia ....................................................

revolución ....................................................

tumulto ....................................................

organizar ....................................................

militante ....................................................

## C. THINGS TO TALK ABOUT

Think about the following. Discuss them with your friends or other people you are studying with.

1. People treated José Ángel's family differently after his father died. How do you think this made him feel? How did it affect his actions in the future?

2. Some people think José Ángel is too militant. Others feel he is working for a good cause. What do you think, and why do you think so?

3. Do you believe there is a need for a political party such as La Raza Unida? What do you think it can accomplish?

36

Denver Post

*Modern Crusader*

# Rodolfo "Corky" Gonzales

Corky Gonzales is a man of many interests. He won the National Amateur Championship as a featherweight boxer before he was twenty years old. He is also a poet, a playwright, and an important political leader. Some people know him as a fierce fighter. However, his wife Geraldine says, "Rodolfo is a gentle man."

Corky was born in a *barrio* in Denver, Colorado, in 1928. His parents were Mexican migrant farm workers. Corky's mother died when he was very young, and his brothers and sisters had to take care of him.

Every spring and summer, the young boy went with his father to harvest sugar beets in the fields of southern Colorado. During the fall and winter, he went to school and worked.

Soon Corky became interested in boxing. He won both the National and International Amateur championships. Then he became a professional. He won sixty-five out of seventy-five professional fights and was rated as the third top contender for the World Featherweight title. Many young Mexican Americans looked to him as a hero.

One night Corky was going to fight in New Orleans. He was standing at a corner near the building where the fight was to be held. An immigration officer came up to him and started asking him questions. Corky had a hard time convincing him that he was a citizen of the United States. Finally he had to point to his picture on the poster that told about his fight.

Although he was successful as a boxer, Corky decided to quit. He felt that he wanted a different kind of life.

Corky tried many careers. He worked as a field laborer, a lumberjack, and an insurance salesperson. After much work, he acquired a large automobile insurance agency and a surety-bond business. He became a success in the world of business.

Corky also entered the world of politics. He became very active in the Democratic party in Denver. In 1960 he participated in the "Viva Kennedy" campaign in Colorado.

BYERS LIBRARY
675 Santa Fe
Denver, Colorado 80204

Besides these activities, he participated in many anti-poverty programs which were designed to help Mexican Americans. However, he began to feel that many of these programs failed to help people. Much money was spent unwisely and much was wasted.

Corky faced a difficult decision. "I was just being used by the politicians," he recalls. "The poor were just as poor." He resigned from the programs and from the Democratic party.

Corky wanted an organization that really helped Mexican Americans. He felt that Chicanos in Denver received unjust treatment from the police, the courts, the welfare department, and the schools.

In 1965 he organized the Crusade for Justice to deal with these issues. Corky and members of the Crusade pushed for many reforms, including bilingual education.

The Crusade also acquired a community center with an auditorium for plays and meetings, a ballroom, a Mexican gift shop, a library, a gym, and a nursery. It opened in September 1969 with a celebration in honor of Mexican Independence Day.

Besides his work with the Crusade, Corky has written several plays and poems. His most popular poem is *Yo Soy Joaquín.* Corky describes his epic poem as a "search for my people's and for my own identity." The poem is about the struggles and achievements of Mexicans and Mexican Americans—past and present.

In speaking of his poem, Gonzales said, "*Yo Soy Joaquín* had to be shared with all my *hermanos y hermanas*, fathers, mothers, and grandparents. Their

time, and now our time, could not be left behind and forgotten."

Corky helped establish *Escuela Tlatelolco.*

Corky's wife and their eight children have also joined him in his efforts to help Chicanos. They helped establish *Escuela Tlatelolco*, the first all-Chicano school in the United States.

In 1969 Corky Gonzales helped set up the National Chicano Youth Conference in Denver. The conference established *El Plan Espiritual de Aztlán. Aztlán* is the land from where the Aztecs began their journey to Mexico City. The goal of the plan is to bring Chicanos together with a new sense of pride in their Mexican heritage. Today Corky is often associated with this idea of *Aztlán.*

Despite many accomplishments, Corky has been a controversial figure. Some people think his ideas are too radical. They believe his plan of *Aztlán* calls for the isolation of Chicanos from American society. Other people feel that Corky has done much to help his people.

# A. UNDERSTANDING THE STORY

Read each of the following carefully. Then select the correct answer from the choices. Write the letter of the correct answer in the blank that follows each.

1. Besides being a fighter, Corky Gonzales is known as a (a) painter, (b) farm worker, (c) poet. ............

2. To many Mexican American youths, Corky, the boxer, was a (a) gentle man, (b) hero, (c) man of many interests. ............

3. After Corky stopped boxing, he became very active in (a) wrestling, (b) business and politics, (c) acting and singing. ............

4. Corky resigned from many anti-poverty programs because he (a) felt they were not really helping people, (b) wanted to enter politics, (c) wanted to write poetry. ............

5. The Crusade for Justice fought against (a) unjust treatment of Chicanos, (b) anti-poverty programs, (c) bilingual education. ............

6. Corky's most famous poem is (a) *Hermanos y Hermanas*, (b) *Yo Soy Joaquín*, (c) *El Plan de Aztlán*. ............

7. *Escuela Tlatelolco* is (a) the first bilingual school in the country, (b) the first all-Chicano school in the United States, (c) a school for teaching migrant farm workers. ............

8. Despite his accomplishments, Corky Gonzales is (a) a controversial figure, (b) recognized by few people, (c) disliked by most people. ............

# B. VOCABULARY

The following words were used in the story. Write a short definition for each word or words that matches its use in the story. Use a dictionary if necessary.

surety bond ...................................................................................................

.................................................................................................................

fierce .........................................................................................................

.................................................................................................................

reform ........................................................................................................

.................................................................................................................

playwright ...................................................................................................

.................................................................................................................

crusade .................................................................................................................

.................................................................................................................

amateur .................................................................................................................

.................................................................................................................

associate .................................................................................................................

.................................................................................................................

epic .................................................................................................................

.................................................................................................................

isolation .................................................................................................................

.................................................................................................................

controversial .................................................................................................................

.................................................................................................................

## C. THINGS TO TALK ABOUT

Think about the following. Discuss them with your friends or other people you are studying with.

1. How do you think Corky felt when he was questioned by an immigration officer before his fight in New Orleans?

2. What do you think about Corky's reasons for resigning from the anti-poverty programs and the Democratic party?

3. What do you think about the idea of establishing a community center and an all-Chicano school? What purposes can they serve?

Private Stock Records

*Texas Troubadour*

# Trini López

From the slums of Dallas's "Little Mexico" to the stages of Hollywood and Las Vegas—this is the road Trini López traveled on the way to sucess. Trini's records have sold millions of copies. His songs have been heard and enjoyed all over the world.

Music has always been part of Trini's life. When he was eleven years old, his father bought him a guitar for twelve dollars and taught him to play. One reason his father taught him to play was to keep him from running with local gangs. "I was raised in a ghetto in Dallas that is composed of blacks and Mexican Americans. It was a tough neighborhood," the singer remembers.

Being able to afford even the twelve dollars for the guitar was not easy for Trini's father. He worked as a janitor in a Dallas hotel and as a gardener on his days off. He had six children to feed and a one-room house to pay for. "You can't imagine how hard it was," Trini recalls.

With his father's encouragement, Trini was soon playing and singing like a professional. After a while, he was playing with a group. They played and sang in restaurants in the *barrio*. Soon they became popular enough to play in night clubs and to travel to other towns.

Trini's mother and father spoke Spanish at home. Trini learned English when he entered school. However, the young student had to drop out of high school.

"I quit in my junior year to help the family," the singer recalls. "I was the oldest, and it was my choice to help out." However, he saw to it that his brother Jesse finished high school and went on to earn a college degree.

Trini knew that to earn "big money" and to be a success he would have to go to Hollywood. His group's Tex-Mex style of rock-and-roll music was popular in the Southwest. However, he felt that a Mexican American had little chance of real success in the area.

In 1960 Trini headed for Hollywood with three hundred dollars in his pocket. He auditioned for the manager of the Ye Little Club. The manager signed him to perform for two weeks, but Trini was so popular that he stayed a year.

Trini was still looking for his big break. He started performing at P.J.'s, a popular club in Hollywood. One night Don Costa, who arranged music for Frank Sinatra, heard Trini sing. Don signed the singer to make a record for Reprise Records, a company owned by Sinatra.

"I had admired Frank Sinatra since I was a young boy," Trini says. "I never dreamed I would be working for him one day or be his friend."

The song Trini recorded was "If I Had a Hammer." In two months it was number one in the nation. It also became the top song in twenty other countries. Over four and a half million copies were sold in the United States alone.

Trini included "If I Had a Hammer" in his first album. The album also included two of his Mexican favorites, "La Bamba" and "Granada."

During his first foreign tour, Trini was a hit everywhere he sang. He played in front of huge crowds every night in Paris. Princess Grace invited him to play for a benefit party in Monte Carlo. The boy from the *barrios* of Dallas had made it to the bigtime.

Now Trini could afford to send money home to help his family. He bought his family a comfortable house and bought his father a car so that he could drive to work.

Trini moved to New York to play at a club called Basin Street East. His orchestra then had eleven members. His brother Jesse had joined the group and was playing the drums. Again Trini was

a hit. He played in many more clubs, and each time he was a tremendous success.

Soon Trini was making movies. He made *Marriage on the Rocks* with Dean Martin and Trini's boyhood idol, Frank Sinatra. Then he played the leading role in the movie *Antonio*.

Trini is very proud of his Mexican American background. "I love my heritage," Trini says, "and I'm proud to be a Mexican American." He has often sung at benefits for various causes to help Mexican Americans. He once joined Vikki Carr at a benefit to help set up a scholarship fund at Southern Methodist University, where his father works.

One year the people of Dallas elected Trini their "Man of the Year." Trini said of his success, "I wanted it. I worked hard. I got it. Your dreams can come true."

## A. UNDERSTANDING THE STORY

Read each of the following carefully. Then select the correct answer from the choices. Write the letter of the correct answer in the blank that follows each.

1. One of the reasons Trini's father bought him a guitar was (a) so that Trini could play music with a local gang, (b) to keep

Trini away from local gangs, (c) so that Trini could play and earn money to help the family. ..............

2. Trini's father (a) worked mostly as a gardener, (b) had seven children to feed and a two-room house to pay for, (c) worked as a janitor in a hotel. ..............

3. The reason Trini left school was to (a) take guitar lessons, (b) help his family, (c) work in a factory. ..............

4. Trini left Texas because (a) his group's Tex-Mex style of rock and roll music was not popular, (b) Don Costa asked him to come to Hollywood, (c) he felt he had little chance of real success in Texas. ..............

5. Trini's big break came when (a) Frank Sinatra heard him sing, (b) the manager of the Ye Little Club signed him to perform, (c) he signed to make a record for Reprise Records. ..............

6. The first record that Trini made was (a) "La Bamba," (b) "If I Had a Hammer," (c) "Granada." ..............

7. Trini had the leading role in (a) *Antonio*, (b) *Marriage on the Rocks*, (c) *Basin Street East*. ..............

8. Trini says he is proud to be (a) a big star, (b) from Dallas, (c) a Mexican American. ..............

## B. VOCABULARY

A synonym is a word having the same or almost the same meaning as another word. Match these words with their synonyms by writing them in the blanks.

slum            comfortable        tough
leading         arrange            huge
admire          earn               popular

1. large      ....................................................

2. pleasant   ....................................................

3. ghetto     ....................................................

4. gain       ....................................................

5. chief      ....................................................

6. rugged     ....................................................

7. respect    ....................................................

8. well-liked ....................................................

9. prepare    ....................................................

## C. THINGS TO WRITE ABOUT

Answer the following questions on the lines provided.

1. Trini had to quit school to help his family. What can be done to prevent young people from having to do this?

.................................................................................................................................

.................................................................................................................................

.................................................................................................................................

.................................................................................................................................

.................................................................................................................................

.................................................................................................................................

.................................................................................................................................

2. Can you give some examples that show Trini's love for his family? Can you give some examples that show his pride in being a Mexican American?

.................................................................................................................................

.................................................................................................................................

.................................................................................................................................

.................................................................................................................................

.................................................................................................................................

.................................................................................................................................

.................................................................................................................................

3. What do you think of Trini's statement that if you work hard, your dreams can come true?

.................................................................................................................................

.................................................................................................................................

.................................................................................................................................

.................................................................................................................................

.................................................................................................................................

.................................................................................................................................

# Grace Gil Olivárez

Grace Gil Olivárez dropped out of high school at the end of her junior year. Twenty years later she entered Notre Dame University, and in 1970 she became the first woman to graduate from the university's law school. It was difficult for a divorced mother with a young son to make it through law school. "I never thought of giving up," she remembers, "but I often thought I wouldn't make it."

Grace was born in Sonora, a small mining town in Arizona. Her father was Spanish, and her mother was both Mexican and Irish. When her parents divorced, she moved to Phoenix with her mother and sisters. The city's high school was so large that the young girl was afraid to go to school. "I panicked," she recalls. "I told my mother I would rather enter a convent." Instead she went to business school and later took and passed the GED exam.

However, she still remembers her school years and the confusion of being a Mexican American in an Anglo culture. "You were taught in school that you mustn't speak Spanish," she recalls. "Then you went home and your parents said, 'You must speak Spanish because the Mexican heritage is rich.' "

Grace also recalls that her teachers taught all children that a typical breakfast is made up of eggs, juice, and bacon. Many Mexican American children eat tortillas and beans for breakfast. One of the ideas she always stresses in both Anglo and Mexican American groups is the need for a better understanding of both cultures.

The Korean war brought hard times to Grace. She lost her job. She had to take odd jobs until she found a job with an advertising agency. Then one day a radio announcer did not show up for a program. Grace filled in. She was such a success that she soon had her own early morning program, "Hora de los Teen-agers."

After that Grace had a job with KIFN, a Spanish-language radio station. "I became the 'Dear Abby' of the Mexican community," she recalls. Her programs dealt with subjects from children to cooking, from sports to community affairs. She also began working with groups that wanted to help Mexican Americans.

Soon Grace became interested in the civil rights movement. She met Father Theodore Hesburgh of Notre Dame University, who was with the Civil Rights Commission. Father Hesburgh helped her get into law school at Notre Dame.

Later Grace took the bar exam and became a lawyer. She has always been glad that she worked for her law degree. "We must all deal with the law," she says, "either to change it or to strengthen it. Before we can do that, we must understand the law."

After she graduated, Grace went to work as director of Arizona's State Office of Economic Opportunity. She also worked on other projects dealing with poverty, population growth, food, and unemployment.

In 1972 she became director of the Institute for Social Research and Development at the University of New Mexico. She was the first woman to have such an important job at the university. This multi-million-dollar program dealt with problems of education, recreation, criminal justice, and economic development. By working in this program, Grace was able to help many people.

Grace is especially interested in helping Mexican Americans. She says, "We want to help ourselves, but we just want the opportunity." She believes that Mexican Americans should be allowed to keep that part of their culture that is beneficial.

Grace Olivárez is particularly concerned with improving the opportunities of Mexican American women. She understands the many problems they have, especially in finding jobs.

The future of New Mexico is important to Grace Olivárez. She says that she would like to see her state become a leader in dealing with problems of population, environment, and poverty. Now that Grace has been appointed director of the State Planning Office, she is in a good position to help accomplish these things.

Grace Olivárez at Her Desk in the New Mexico State Planning Office

## A. UNDERSTANDING THE STORY

Read each of the following carefully. Then select the correct answer from the choices. Write the letter of the correct answer in the blank that follows each.

1. Grace Olivárez dropped out of high school at the end of her
   (a) freshman year, (b) first semester, (c) junior year.

   ............

2. When Grace was in law school, she often thought (a) of giving up, (b) of nothing but books, (c) she wouldn't make it. ............

3. Grace was confused in high school because (a) the school was so large, (b) she was very young, (c) she was a Mexican American in an Anglo culture. ............

4. Father Theodore Hesburgh helped Grace (a) with her work at the Civil Rights Commission, (b) obtain work at a radio station, (c) enter law school. ............

5. According to Grace, people must understand the law in order to (a) change or strengthen it, (b) become better citizens, (c) work as directors of multi-million-dollar programs. ............

6. Grace Olivárez was one of the first women to (a) graduate from the University of New Mexico, (b) hold a very important position at the University of Notre Dame, (c) hold a very high office at the University of New Mexico. ............

7. According to Grace, Mexican Americans should be allowed to (a) keep that part of their culture that is beneficial, (b) speak Spanish, (c) change their Spanish names. ............

8. Grace is particularly concerned with the problem Mexican American women have in (a) the area of education, (b) finding jobs, (c) the area of public health. ............

## B. VOCABULARY

Match each word in Column A with its meaning in Column B by writing the letter of the meaning in the blank in front of the word.

| | Column A | | Column B |
|---|---|---|---|
| ............ | 1. difficult | a. | helpful |
| ............ | 2. panic | b. | handled |
| ............ | 3. confusion | c. | hard |
| ............ | 4. heritage | d. | act of improving |
| ............ | 5. typical | e. | the state of not being able to think clearly, disorder |
| ............ | 6. stresses | f. | something handed down from the past |
| ............ | 7. dealt (with) | g. | being a true example of its kind |
| ............ | 8. development | h. | to have fear so great as to lose self control |
| ............ | 9. beneficial | i. | remember |
| ............ | 10. recall | j. | gives importance to |

# C. THINGS TO WRITE ABOUT

Answer the following questions on the lines provided.

1. Grace thought the high school in Phoenix was very large. How did that make her feel?

.....................................................................................................................

.....................................................................................................................

.....................................................................................................................

.....................................................................................................................

.....................................................................................................................

.....................................................................................................................

.....................................................................................................................

2. Grace stresses the need for better understanding between Anglos and Mexican Americans. How do you feel about this? Why do you feel the way you do?

.....................................................................................................................

.....................................................................................................................

.....................................................................................................................

.....................................................................................................................

.....................................................................................................................

.....................................................................................................................

.....................................................................................................................

3. Grace says Mexican Americans should be allowed to keep that part of their culture which is beneficial. Do you think this should apply to any minority group? Why?

.....................................................................................................................

.....................................................................................................................

.....................................................................................................................

.....................................................................................................................

.....................................................................................................................

.....................................................................................................................

.....................................................................................................................

Markow Photography

*American by Choice*

# Raul H. Castro

In January 1975 Raul H. Castro moved into the Arizona statehouse to begin his term as governor. The road to the governor's office was a long, hard one for Castro. He lost his first governor's race in 1970 by a small number of votes.

Raul Castro was born on June 12, 1916, in Cananea, Mexico. His family was very poor. Raul's parents and their fourteen children lived in a one-room hut. When Raul was a small boy, the family moved to Douglas, Arizona.

Raul began working when he was nine years old. He took every odd job he could find. However, he seldom missed a day of school. Early in his life, Raul had decided that education and hard work were the ways to get ahead in life.

Learning was somewhat difficult at first for Raul. "During my early years in school," he remembers, "I discovered I was at a great handicap in comparison to Mexican Americans born in this country, as well as to the Anglo students." Raul did not give up, however. In time he graduated from high school and went on to college.

In order to afford college, Raul had to work part-time as a farmhand, a rancher, and a miner. He graduated from Northern Arizona University.

Castro developed a deep love for the United States and his adopted state of Arizona. However, he waited until he had graduated from college to become a naturalized citizen of the United States. He wanted to be sure he "could contribute to the growth and success of the country."

Castro became a teacher in an elementary school. Teaching brought out in him a desire for even more education. However, World War II began. Castro left his job and served as an official in the United States Foreign Service.

When the war was over, Raul made up his mind to become a lawyer. He taught Spanish at the University of Arizona to pay his way through law school.

After graduation he worked as a lawyer for five years. In 1955 Castro became the first county attorney of Mexican origin in the history of Arizona's Pima County.

Four years later he was elected judge of the Superior Court. Then he served as judge of the Juvenile Court. Castro earned the respect of many people for the fair treatment he gave the young people he faced.

One person who heard about Raul Castro was President Lyndon Johnson. In 1964 he sent Castro to El Salvador as the ambassador from the United States. The people of El Salvador were so pleased with Castro's service that they gave him their country's highest award, the Matias Delgado Decoration. Then President Johnson named Castro the ambassador to Bolivia.

When Castro returned to the United States, he decided to run for governor of Arizona. He ran against the governor in office and lost by a few votes.

Castro remembered the words of his mother: "Because one door has been closed to you does not mean all people think that way. Another door can open tomorrow."

For the next four years, Castro visited with the people of Arizona. He wanted to learn their needs and to introduce himself to them. He said, "If you're not determined to succeed, then you will drift without aim and become a failure." In

Castro with One of His Prize Horses at the Castro Ranch

November 1974 he was elected governor.

Governor Castro stands as a symbol of the opportunities his state offers all people. "I think my election has shown that Mexican Americans can be accepted and can succeed in any endeavor in which they care to make an effort."

"I love people," Castro says. "From every person I have known, I have learned. From every person I have worked with, I have grown. Arizona has great beauty—in her mountains and deserts and canyons and wildlife—but the greatest beauty of Arizona is her people."

## A. UNDERSTANDING THE STORY

Read each of the following carefully. Then select the correct answer from the choices. Write the letter of the correct answer in the blank that follows each.

1. Early in his life, Raul Castro decided that the way to get ahead in life was (a) through politics, (b) by becoming a United States citizen, (c) through education and hard work.

............

2. In school Castro was handicapped in comparison to (a) Mexican Americans born in the United States, (b) Indians, (c) other Mexican students. ............

3. Castro developed a deep love for (a) the law, (b) the United States, (c) teaching. ............

4. When World War II was over, Castro decided to (a) run for governor, (b) teach in an elementary school, (c) become a lawyer. ............

5. Many people respected Castro as a judge because of the fair treatment he gave to (a) young people, (b) Mexican Americans, (c) Anglos. ............

6. After Castro lost an election for governor, he was encouraged by the words (a) of President Lyndon Johnson, (b) of his mother, (c) written on the Matias Delgado Decoration. ............

7. According to Governor Castro, his election has shown that (a) naturalized citizens can succeed in their endeavors, (b) Mexican Americans can succeed in their endeavors, (c) he was the best person for that office. ............

8. Castro says that Arizona's greatest beauty is her (a) deserts, (b) people, (c) wildlife. ............

## B. VOCABULARY

An antonym is a word which has the opposite meaning of another word. Match these words with their antonyms by writing them in the blanks.

| | | |
|---|---|---|
| seldom | pleased | failure |
| handicap | desire | accepted |
| fair | respect | |

1. rejected .................................................................

2. advantage .................................................................

3. success .................................................................

4. repulsion .................................................................

5. disappointed .................................................................

6. always .................................................................

7. disrespect .................................................................

8. unjust .................................................................

# C. THINGS TO WRITE ABOUT

Answer the following questions on the lines provided.

1. Castro says that school was more difficult for him than for native-born Mexican Americans or Anglos. What can be done to help people who come from a foreign country and have difficulty in school?

..................................................................................................................

..................................................................................................................

..................................................................................................................

..................................................................................................................

..................................................................................................................

..................................................................................................................

2. Why does Raul Castro stand as a symbol of the opportunities his state offers all people?

..................................................................................................................

..................................................................................................................

..................................................................................................................

..................................................................................................................

..................................................................................................................

..................................................................................................................

3. What do you think Castro means when he says, "If you're not determined to succeed, then you will drift without aim and become a failure"?

..................................................................................................................

..................................................................................................................

..................................................................................................................

..................................................................................................................

..................................................................................................................

..................................................................................................................

# Jerry Apodaca

On New Year's Day, 1975, Jerry Apodaca became governor of the state of New Mexico. It was a great achievement for Jerry. He became the first governor of Spanish origin in over fifty years.

Jerry Apodaca is proud that he has both a Spanish and a Mexican heritage. The name "Apodaca" originated in Spain. Jerry's ancestors came to the United States from Mexico. "I was raised in a Mexican neighborhood," Governor Apodaca says. "Now it is called a *barrio*. The term 'Chicano' is not a new one for me. It was used in my neighborhood when I was a boy."

Jerry Apodaca was born in Las Cruces, New Mexico, in 1934. He went to high school there and then on to college at the University of New Mexico.

College was sometimes difficult for Jerry. "When things got me down, athletics kept me going," he remembers. He was a star football player for the university. Today he plays football in the backyard with his sons. "I still get a kick out of playing football, jogging, and skiing," he says.

After graduation Jerry married a pretty cheerleader, Clara Melendres. He taught history and coached football at Albuquerque Valley High School. Since it was difficult to make ends meet, Jerry often had to work at night to supplement his meager salary.

Jerry's wife also worked to help support the family. She used to monitor

*New Mexico Magazine*

Jerry Apodaca and His Sons Jogging

television commercials. "She was the only one I ever heard of who watched all the commercials and went to the bathroom during the programs," Jerry says.

In 1961 Jerry decided to leave teaching and enter the world of business. Jerry and Clara opened their own insurance business in their hometown of Las Cruces. Their desk was just a wooden table. All papers were stored on top of this table because they couldn't afford a file cabinet.

Jerry and his wife worked hard to get started. Soon, however, their efforts paid off. They acquired two shoe stores and a real estate company, in addition to their insurance company. Jerry became a board member of the Citizen's Bank in Las Cruces.

Jerry Apodaca believes that the secret of any success is dedication. He dedicated himself to teaching and then to becoming a success in the business world.

Next he dedicated himself to politics. He entered politics by helping another candidate, Jack Campbell, in his race for the governor's office. In 1964 Jerry ran for the state senate and lost. He vowed never to run again. However, in 1966 he ran again and won.

Jerry's teaching experience helped him in the legislature. He served as head of the Legislative School Study Committee. He helped to pass many laws providing for special education, vocational education, preschool programs, and bilingual education.

Then, in 1975 he became governor of his state. Now his mind is on the needs of his state. "I want to put New Mexico on the map," he says. "I want to make the rest of the world know we're here."

He is also concerned with helping Mexican Americans. One of his goals is to keep the door open for other Mexican Americans to run for office. "President Kennedy helped open the door for candidates of any religion," he says. "I would like to open it for Mexican Americans. It hasn't been open for over fifty years. I'd like to be sure that it isn't closed for one hundred years."

Jerry hopes that his struggle will serve as an example for other Mexican Americans. Now that Jerry Apodaca has achieved success, other Mexican Americans know they can succeed, too.

## A. UNDERSTANDING THE STORY

Read each of the following carefully. Then select the correct answer from the choices. Write the letter of the correct answer in the blank that follows each.

1. Jerry Apodaca is New Mexico's first governor of Spanish origin in (a) over one hundred years, (b) over fifty years, (c) this century. ............

2. Jerry grew up in (a) Spain, (b) a *barrio* in Mexico, (c) a *barrio* in Las Cruces. ............

3. Jerry often had to work at night (a) because his pay as a teacher was small, (b) so he could afford a file cabinet, (c) because the Apodacas wanted to buy a shoe store. ............

4. The first business the Apodacas owned was (a) a shoe store, (b) a real estate company, (c) an insurance agency.   ............

5. Jerry feels that he and his wife were successful in business because of (a) luck, (b) dedication, (c) help from friends.   ............

6. Jerry was able to help pass many useful laws on education because of his (a) coaching experience, (b) teaching experience, (c) bilingual background.   ............

7. Jerry Apodaca is concerned about (a) the maps of New Mexico, (b) his next election, (c) the needs of his state.   ............

8. One of Jerry Apodaca's concerns is that (a) more people from different religious groups should run for office, (b) more people from different minority groups should run for office, (c) fewer people should run for office.   ............

## B. VOCABULARY

The following words were used in the story. Write a short definition for each word that matches its use in the story. Use a dictionary if necessary.

ancestor .................................................................................................

.............................................................................................................

meager ..................................................................................................

.............................................................................................................

originate ................................................................................................

.............................................................................................................

supplement ...........................................................................................

.............................................................................................................

afford ....................................................................................................

.............................................................................................................

vow .......................................................................................................

.............................................................................................................

candidate ..............................................................................................

.............................................................................................................

monitor ..................................................................................................

.............................................................................................................

## C. THINGS TO WRITE ABOUT

Answer the following questions on the lines provided.

1. Jerry Apodaca believes the secret of any success is dedication. Can you give some examples that show his dedication?

.........................................................................................................................

.........................................................................................................................

.........................................................................................................................

.........................................................................................................................

.........................................................................................................................

.........................................................................................................................

.........................................................................................................................

2. How did Jerry's teaching experience help him in the legislature? How do you think his experience in business might help him as governor?

.........................................................................................................................

.........................................................................................................................

.........................................................................................................................

.........................................................................................................................

.........................................................................................................................

.........................................................................................................................

.........................................................................................................................

.........................................................................................................................

3. Do you think Clara Apodaca's help contributed to Jerry Apodaca's success? How?

.........................................................................................................................

.........................................................................................................................

.........................................................................................................................

.........................................................................................................................

.........................................................................................................................

.........................................................................................................................

.........................................................................................................................

Lee Treviño Enterprises, Inc.

*The Story of a Champion*

# Lee Treviño

When the name Lee Treviño is mentioned to any group in the city of El Paso, Texas, the crowd roars and cheers. The city's "singing policeman," Ramón Rendón, often sings "Que Viva Lee Treviño," the song that tells the story of the champion. Lee Treviño is indeed a champion and a hero to many.

Golf has always been a part of Lee's life. He and his two sisters grew up with their mother and grandfather in a house near Dallas, Texas. Their home had only four rooms and no electricity or plumbing. However, it was near the Glen Lakes Golf Course. Lee often chased balls for the golfers. He watched and dreamed that someday he too would hit the ball down the fairway just as they did.

"It was a lonely life," Lee says. "I was never around anybody."

One day when he was six years old, Lee found a left-handed golf club in a hayfield. He was right-handed, but the club was his. He turned it around and began hitting balls. Every day Lee searched for another golf club. Soon he found one—and it was a right-handed one. He dug out two holes in the hayfield and made his own golf course. Lee practiced and practiced.

Lee had to quit school in the eighth grade. He had to work to help buy food for the family. "I never knew what steak was," Lee says. The best meal his family ate was hash and baloney, washed down with Kool-Aid.

When Lee was old enough, he joined the marines. He made new friends, and he liked the duties and responsibilities. "It was like camping out," Lee remembers. "It was the best time of my life. I got my sense of humor when I was in the marines."

Lee also got a chance to play golf. One day he saw a notice on the bulletin board. The Third Marine Division was holding tryouts for a golf team. "Shucks, I know a little about that game," Lee said to himself. He asked his commanding officer to let him try out for the team. The officer decided to take on Lee himself. Lee beat him and went on to beat the entire division team. When he left the Marine Corps two years later, Lee was determined to become a professional golfer.

Lee returned to Dallas and began working at Hardy Greenwood's driving range and pitch-and-putt course. He ran the golf shop and soon became Mr. Greenwood's right-hand man. More important, Lee was playing golf every chance he could get.

Lee even played trick golf with some of the players at Tenison Park Municipal Golf Course. He would wrap adhesive tape around a soft drink bottle and use it for a club. "I used a Dr Pepper bottle because it is smooth, while a Coke bottle is rough," Lee says. He usually made his shot.

With the help of a friend, Lee entered the Texas State Open in Houston in 1965—and won. He finished second in the Mexican Open in the same year.

Treviño made up his mind that he would begin touring as a professional. By now he had quit his job in Dallas and had moved to El Paso. Entering the professional golf tour was a big risk, but Lee had to try.

In 1967 he was accepted as a member of the Professional Golf Association. Since Lee had played so poorly in the U.S. Open the year before, he was afraid that he was not ready.

Lee's wife, Claudia, sent in the twenty-dollar entry fee for the U.S. Open and told Lee he must go. Lee was very nervous. He ate peaches and plums in his motel room to keep himself going. He shot the lowest score in the qualifying rounds, and then finished fifth in the Open. Lee was on his way to the top.

The next year, Lee tied Jack Nicklaus's all-time low scoring record to win the U.S. Open. From then on it was one tournament victory after another—the Hawaiian Open, the Tucson Open, the World Cup, and many more. Lee soon ranked as one of the "big money" winners, along with such golfers as Arnold Palmer, Billy Casper, Jack Nicklaus, and Gary Player.

Lee Treviño Enterprises, Inc.

However, Lee's career has not been all winning. In 1970 he missed several putts at the Colonial in Fort Worth and lost to Homero Blancas. "I never thought I'd get beat by a Mexican," said Lee, laughing.

Win or lose, Lee Treviño is always a good sport. "I don't complain about anything, because I love golf," he says. "I love to travel, and I love to make people laugh."

When his playing hit a slump, Lee began to practice extra hard. He was out on the golf course early, and he came home late. His practice paid off. Soon he was winning again. In 1971 *Sports Illustrated* magazine named him Sportsman of the Year. They called him "a common man with an uncommon touch."

Many people know Lee Treviño's friendly face from the television commercials he has done. He has given much money to various charities, and many poor and sick people have come to call him friend. "I'm concerned with the poor—black, white, yellow, red—and the young," he says. He remembers the hard times he experienced when he was just starting.

Those times, however, are now over. Lee Treviño has found success. The boy with the left-handed club has become one of golf's great players.

## A. UNDERSTANDING THE STORY

Read each of the following carefully. Then select the correct answer from the choices. Write the letter of the correct answer in the blank that follows each.

1. Lee describes his childhood as being (a) filled with poverty, (b) lonely, (c) very happy. ............

2. Lee started practicing golf when he (a) found a club in a hay-field, (b) joined the marines, (c) quit school. ............

3. In the marines Lee (a) learned how to play professional golf, (b) was very unhappy, (c) got his sense of humor. ............

4. At Tenison Park Municipal Golf Course, Lee often played (a) trick golf, (b) professional golf, (b) amateur golf. ............

5. Lee was afraid to begin touring as a professional because he played poorly at the (a) Texas State Open, (b) U.S. Open, (c) Mexican Open. ............

6. The person who helped Lee join the professional golf tour was (a) Jack Nicklaus, (b) Hardy Greenwood, (c) his wife Claudia. ............

7. When Lee's playing hit a slump, he (a) considered giving up, (b) started taking lessons, (c) began to practice more. ............

8. Many poor and sick people like Lee because he (a) makes them laugh, (b) has a friendly face, (c) has donated much money to charities. ............

## B. VOCABULARY

A synonym is a word having the same or almost the same meanings as another word. Match these words with their synonyms by writing them in the blanks.

| lonely | notice | rank |
|--------|--------|------|
| roars | wrap | slump |
| duties | risk | |

1. cover ...............................................................

2. solitary ...............................................................

3. announcement ...............................................................

4. decline ...............................................................

5. gamble ...............................................................

6. screams ...............................................................

7. classify ...............................................................

8. obligations ...............................................................

## C. THINGS TO WRITE ABOUT

Answer the following questions on the lines provided.

1. What qualities did Lee have that helped make him a success?

..................................................................................................................

..................................................................................................................

..................................................................................................................

..................................................................................................................

..................................................................................................................

..................................................................................................................

..................................................................................................................

2. Do you think Claudia's support was important to Lee? Why?

..................................................................................................................

..................................................................................................................

..................................................................................................................

..................................................................................................................

..................................................................................................................

..................................................................................................................

..................................................................................................................

3. Lee says he is concerned with the poor. How has he shown his concern?

..................................................................................................................

..................................................................................................................

..................................................................................................................

..................................................................................................................

..................................................................................................................

..................................................................................................................

# Mari-Luci Jaramillo

Obtaining an education was a great financial struggle for Mari-Luci Jaramillo. When she was a student in college, a teacher lent her two hundred dollars to help her finish her education. The teacher, Nell Doherty, told Mari-Luci to repay the loan only if she could. Doherty told Mari-Luci that if she couldn't pay the loan, perhaps she could later help some other students.

Mari-Luci graduated from college with honors. She repaid the loan and helped many other students as well. She dedicated her life to the field of education.

Mari-Luci decided to become a teacher when she was just a young girl growing up in Las Vegas, New Mexico. Although she began school without being able to speak, read, or write English, she was soon an excellent student. Early each morning, Mari-Luci kept warm and studied by the light of a kerosene lamp.

Studying paid off for the young girl. She graduated at the head of her class and received many awards. However, she received no scholarships for a college education. Still, Mari-Luci was de-termined that she would go to college.

She worked in her father's shoe repair shop and saved her money. Then she enrolled at New Mexico Highlands University. She remained there for one year until she used all her savings.

To complete her education, Mari-Luci began a cycle of work and study. She attended school one semester and worked at a factory during the next semester to make enough money for the following year. Nell Doherty's loan of two hundred dollars helped her finish college.

After graduation Mari-Luci began teaching. She found her work interesting and rewarding. She remembers one of her experiences while teaching in the third grade. She asked a pupil, "Do you have trouble reading?"

The child answered, "Oh, no, I only have trouble with the words."

While Mari-Luci was teaching, she attended night classes at Highlands University. She obtained her master's degree and moved to Albuquerque, New Mexico, to teach in a *barrio* school.

After a few months, Mari-Luci became

the assistant director of Latin American Educational Programs at the University of New Mexico. Her job took her to many countries in Central and South America. She met many people and had many interesting experiences during her trips.

Mari-Luci noticed that other Mexican American women were obtaining important jobs in which they could help many people. "The Chicana has become very vocal about what she wants and what she needs," she feels. "She is helping all minority people in their quest for equality." Mari-Luci wanted to become more involved in helping people, too.

Mari-Luci obtained her doctor's degree from the University of New Mexico and became an associate professor. Soon she became a leading authority in the area of education for Spanish-speaking people. She has written many articles and has given many speeches on the subject.

Today Dr. Mari-Luci Jaramillo continues her work in education. She is particularly active in training teachers for bilingual programs.

Dr. Jaramillo has met many Chicano students through her work. "Chicano youth today are more sure of themselves and more aware of their rights and responsibilities," she says. "They feel that they must help others, including the poor."

Mari-Luci also feels that students today have more opportunities than she had when she was growing up and trying to get an education. "Today more teachers are willing to help Chicanos and to listen to them," she says. "Also more employers are willing to hire them—but still at low paying levels."

According to Dr. Jaramillo, education is one way people can help themselves. "I was lucky in that I had a good basic education," she says. "I also had teachers and professors who encouraged me. If I hadn't gotten a good education, I might be in the same situation many other people are in—a life of poverty."

## A. UNDERSTANDING THE STORY

Read each of the following carefully. Then select the correct answer from the choices. Write the letter of the correct answer in the blank that follows each.

1. Nell Doherty helped Mari-Luci finish college by (a) lending her five hundred dollars, (b) giving her a job, (c) lending her two hundred dollars.

............

2. Mari-Luci decided to become a teacher (a) when she was a young girl growing up in Las Vegas, New Mexico, (b) when she was in college, (c) after graduating from high school.  ............

3. When Mari-Luci graduated from high school, she received (a) a loan of two hundred dollars, (b) many awards, (c) several scholarships to go to college.  ............

4. To get a college education, Mari-Luci attended school one semester and (a) worked in her father's shoe repair shop the next semester, (b) taught in the third grade the next semester, (c) worked in a factory the next semester.  ............

5. While Mari-Luci worked as assistant director of Latin American Educational Programs, she (a) attended night classes, (b) often traveled to South America, (c) worked on obtaining her doctor's degree.  ............

6. Dr. Jaramillo is a leading authority in the area of (a) Chicano rights, (b) education for Spanish-speaking people, (c) Latin American studies.  ............

7. Dr. Jaramillo thinks that Mexican American youth today (a) are more sure of themselves, (b) are very insecure, (c) have fewer opportunities than she had.  ............

8. According to Mari-Luci, one way to avoid a life of poverty is (a) through hard work, (b) through education, (c) by becoming more aware of your rights and responsibilities.  ............

## B. VOCABULARY

The following words were used in the story. Write a short definition for each word that matches its use in the story. Use a dictionary if necessary.

basic ......................................................................................................................

................................................................................................................................

cycle ......................................................................................................................

................................................................................................................................

rewarding ..............................................................................................................

................................................................................................................................

quest ......................................................................................................................

................................................................................................................................

authority ................................................................................................................

................................................................................................................................

semester ...........................................................................................................

...........................................................................................................

scholarship ...........................................................................................................

...........................................................................................................

vocal ...........................................................................................................

...........................................................................................................

financial ...........................................................................................................

...........................................................................................................

responsibility ...........................................................................................................

...........................................................................................................

## C. THINGS TO WRITE ABOUT

Answer the following questions on the lines provided.

1. One of Mari-Luci's problems in obtaining a college education was the lack of money. Today many colleges offer scholarships to help needy students. How do you feel about such scholarships?

...........................................................................................................

...........................................................................................................

...........................................................................................................

...........................................................................................................

...........................................................................................................

2. Marci-Luci feels that today's Chicano youth are more sure of themselves and more aware of their rights and responsibilities. Do you think the same is true of all youth today? Explain.

...........................................................................................................

...........................................................................................................

...........................................................................................................

...........................................................................................................

...........................................................................................................

...........................................................................................................

The University of Texas Institute of Texan Cultures

*Texas's Bluebonnet Painter*

# Porfirio Salinas

Each spring the Texas hill country is covered with a blanket of blue flowers. The bluebonnet is one of Texas's many wild flowers. It has become the state's official flower, and Porfirio Salinas became known as the "bluebonnet painter of Texas."

One story tells that in the 1920s the artist Robert Wood had painted many pictures of the Texas landscape. He said that he could not paint one more bluebonnet. He hired young Porfirio Salinas to paint them for him. Wood agreed to pay Salinas five dollars for each picture.

Porfirio Salinas was born in Bastrop, Texas, in 1910. Later the family moved to San Antonio. There young Porfirio attended school for three years. He quit school to work at odd jobs to help his family.

One of his jobs was with a company that sold art supplies. Famous painters often came in to buy their supplies. As often as possible, Porfirio talked with these artists about their work. Soon he was visiting the Witte Museum in San Antonio to look at the paintings.

Porfirio decided to become a painter. He studied the works of other artists and spent long hours practicing with his brush. Soon he began to earn a little money. He would paint a Christmas card or a scene on a truck. He was not selling many paintings, but he was painting. He had never had an art lesson or gone to an art school.

Many people encouraged the young artist. Among them were the Spanish artist, Jose Arpa, and the landscape painter, Robert Wood. Porfirio often went with them on painting trips into the Texas hill country.

One day the young artist was walking down the street. He was carrying a heavy load of brushes and canvas for his work. He glanced into a window of a railway company office and saw a young and pretty secretary. She returned his look. Porfirio went in and introduced himself to María Bonilla. The young people became close friends. Soon they were married.

Salinas continued to paint the scenes of Texas. He loved the hills of bluebonnets in the spring and the trees with their golden leaves in autumn. He was fascinated with the irregular patterns of cactus that dotted the hillsides. He painted and painted, but he still sold few of his works.

One day Dewey Bradford, an art dealer from Austin, saw one of Salinas's paintings in a store window. It was a painting of Texas cactus. Bradford said to himself, "It's not possible for an amateur to paint a field of cactus. He'd be foolish to try. This fella must be either a genius or crazy."

Bradford entered the shop and bought the painting. He knew good art when he saw it. Bradford asked about the artist and set out to introduce himself to Salinas. The two men soon struck a bargain. Bradford would sell all the pictures that Salinas could paint.

Bradford knew how to sell paintings. He knew many people who would buy the works of Texas artists. One day a rich Texas businessman from Fort Worth, Sid W. Richardson, purchased one of Salinas's paintings. Richardson had grown up in Texas, and he loved the countryside. Richardson gave the paint-

ing to Sam Rayburn, a famous member of Congress from Texas.

Rayburn arranged for the painting to hang in the dining room of the White House. The White House dining room was redecorated to match the colors of the painting. The painting hung in a place of honor until Rayburn died. Now the painting hangs in the Sam Rayburn Library in Bonham, Texas.

In 1940 Lyndon B. Johnson began collecting Salinas's paintings. He hung them in his office and at his Texas ranch. He often gave them as gifts to visitors. When Johnson became vice president of the United States, he had Salinas paint a Texas landscape to give to President John F. Kennedy. The painting was to be presented to the president on the day he was assassinated in Dallas. The painting, entitled "Rocky Creek," is now stored in Dewey Bradford's studio. Salinas could not bear for anyone but the young president to have it.

Salinas's friendship with Lyndon Johnson continued after Johnson became president. Salinas was often a visitor at the LBJ ranch. Salinas's painting, "Autumn in the Hill Country," with its cactus, barbed wire, and oak trees with their orange leaves, was one of the president's favorite paintings.

President Johnson once gave a Salinas painting to López Mateos, the president of Mexico. The present so pleased Mateos that he sent for Salinas and asked the artist to paint some Mexican scenes for his personal collection.

Although Salinas was proud of his success as an artist, he never changed. He still wore simple clothes and kept simple habits.

Many times he closed his studio and took his wife and daughter, María Cristina, to Mexico. There he walked through art museums to study the works of Mexican artists. He painted the bulls and the colorful bullfighters. He

The University of Texas Institute of Texan Cultures

loved to visit the small Mexican villages and paint adobe huts, bright flowers, and people. He often said that he went to Mexico to paint and to "replenish his soul."

There are few stories about Salinas. He never liked to entertain or to tell stories. He was always serious, especially when talking about his art. When people asked why he did not give titles to many of his paintings, he would reply, "Why give them titles? They are whatever they say to the viewer."

Even after his death in 1973, Salinas is recognized as one of the Southwest's most popular artists. His paintings speak to many art lovers. They capture the spirit of the Southwest. Through his bluebonnets, his cactus, his autumn trees, and his scenes of the Texas countryside, many people have learned to appreciate the Texas that Salinas loved.

## A. UNDERSTANDING THE STORY

Read each of the following carefully. Then select the correct answer from the choices. Write the letter of the correct answer in the blank that follows each.

1. The official state flower of Texas is the (a) rose, (b) wild flower, (c) bluebonnet. ............

2. Salinas quit school to (a) earn money for art lessons, (b) help his family, (c) visit the Witte Museum. ............

3. Salinas never had (a) a good paint brush, (b) an art lesson, (c) good health. ............

4. Among the objects that Salinas painted were (a) rocks and birds, (b) roses and pansies, (c) bluebonnets and cactus. ............

5. Salinas began to sell his paintings when (a) he changed his style, (b) Dewey Bradford began to handle his work, (c) the bluebonnet became popular. ............

6. One of the first to buy Salinas's paintings was (a) Lyndon Johnson, (b) Sid Richardson, (c) Sam Rayburn. ............

7. One of President Lyndon B. Johnson's favorite paintings by Salinas is called, (a) "Rocky Creek," (b) "Cactus and Bluebonnets," (c) "Autumn in the Hill Country." ............

8. Salinas's paintings (a) always have titles, (b) capture the spirit of the Southwest, (c) are popular only in Texas. ............

9. Salinas is recognized as one of the most popular artists (a) in the Southwest, (b) in this country, (c) in Mexico. ............

# B. VOCABULARY

Match each word in Column A with its meaning in Column B by writing the letter of the meaning in the blank in front of the word.

| | Column A | | Column B |
|---|---|---|---|
| ............ | 1. purchase | a. | a person who buys and sells things |
| ............ | 2. wild | b. | materials, equipment |
| ............ | 3. dealer | c. | to renew, to restore |
| ............ | 4. supplies | d. | to accept a situation |
| ............ | 5. encourage | e. | view |
| ............ | 6. bear | f. | cloth used for painting on |
| ............ | 7. replenish | g. | not cultivated |
| ............ | 8. canvas | h. | to buy |
| ............ | 9. scene | i. | design, form |
| ............ | 10. pattern | j. | to inspire with hope |

Sometimes an English word is very similar to its Spanish translation. Fill in each blank with a word from the story that matches the Spanish word.

asesinar ..............................................................

apreciar ..............................................................

fascinar ..............................................................

hábito ..............................................................

reconocer ..............................................................

# C. THINGS TO TALK ABOUT

Think about the following. Discuss them with your friends or other people you are studying with.

1. Do you think Salinas contributed to the art of the Southwest?

2. Salinas said that he often went to Mexico to "replenish his soul." What do you think he meant? Do you know any Mexican Americans who feel the same way?

World Wide Photos, Inc.

# Reies López Tijerina

Since the war between Mexico and the United States, there have been much confusion and conflict over the issue of land ownership in the Southwest. In recent times Reies Tijerina has helped bring national attention to this issue.

Reies Tijerina was born in Falls City, Texas, on September 21, 1923. His parents were migrant farm workers. The family followed the migrant stream from the Rio Grande Valley to the Midwest. Reies received very little education, even though he attended over twenty different schools.

One day a Baptist minister visited the migrant camp where the Tijerina family lived. He left a copy of the Bible with the Tijerinas. Reies read it each night before he went to sleep. He soon felt he had a calling from God to help people.

Tijerina left the fields and went to an Assembly of God school near El Paso, Texas, and became a minister. He worked in the fields and preached in migrant camps. Many times he gave away everything he had to people who were in need.

In the early 1950s, Tijerina and a number of families established a village in Arizona and named it *Valle de la Paz*, "Valley of Peace." The group built homes and a church, and they farmed the land. However, trouble soon developed with neighboring farmers. The village was burned, and the people were forced to flee.

Tijerina went to northern New Mexico where he heard the story of the land rights issue. He learned that the war between Mexico and the United States had ended with the Treaty of Guadalupe Hidalgo. This treaty stated that Spanish Americans living in the Southwest were to keep their civil and property rights.

Tijerina learned that some people felt that the treaty had not been honored. The Mexicans of the Southwest, who were now United States citizens, were unfamiliar with the land laws of this country. The use of surveyors, land titles, and even property taxes was new to them. As a result, many families lost their property through complicated legal actions which were totally unfamiliar to them. Some felt they were cheated out of their property. There was much resentment as a result, and the descendants of these people also felt this resentment.

Tijerina spent the next few years investigating and studying the land issue. He became an expert on property rights.

In 1963 Tijerina helped form the *Alianza Federal de Mercedes*, "The Federated Alliance of Land Grants," to help the people regain their land. "The people were totally dependent on this land, physically, morally, spiritually," Tijerina says. "I saw the land question as the hope of the Southwest."

Tijerina and members of the *Alianza* went to various state and federal agencies trying to draw attention to their cause. They wanted an investigation of the land issue. Often they were turned back and denied a chance to present their views.

In October 1966 over three hundred members of the *Alianza* moved into a campground at the Kit Carson National Forest in northern New Mexico. They declared the area the Republic of San Joaquín del Rio de Chama and elected their own mayor and council. There were various confrontations between members of the *Alianza* and Forest Service rangers.

Then in June 1967 eleven members of the *Alianza* were arrested. People in the *Alianza* believed the arrests were made to prevent a mass meeting of the *Alianza* in the village of Coyote, New Mexico.

A few days later, several members of the *Alianza* raided the Tierra Amarilla courthouse and tried to free the prisoners and place the district attorney under citizen's arrest. Again there was a confrontation, and this time several people were wounded.

It is still unclear whether Tijerina participated or not. Tijerina states that he was at a nearby home and later went to the courthouse to stop the activities.

Tijerina defends himself in court.

Others say that he actively participated in the raid. Five days later Tijerina and several other people were arrested and charged with fifty-four different criminal violations.

Tijerina's trial attracted much attention. Instead of hiring a lawyer, Tijerina decided to defend himself. He used the occasion to draw attention once again to the issue of land rights. In December 1968 the jury found Tijerina not guilty.

The trouble did not end, however. There were several incidents of violence after that. Members of the *Alianza* felt that the police and various other law-enforcement agencies were harassing their organization. The legal authorities, on the other hand, accused the *Alianza* of being the cause of the trouble.

In October 1969 Tijerina was sent to jail on a charge of burning a sign in a

National Forest, as well as various other charges. Tijerina remained in jail until July 1971.

Today, the *Alianza* continues its work. There is no longer the turmoil that marked the early years, however. "I have outgrown militancy," Tijerina says.

"I can see beyond it. I want to bring peace and understanding among the people of New Mexico."

The preacher from Texas has drawn much national attention to the land issue. However, the dispute over land rights continues.

## A. UNDERSTANDING THE STORY

Read each of the following carefully. Then select the correct answer from the choices. Write the letter of the correct answer in the blank that follows each.

1. Reies López Tijerina received little education as a child, even though (a) he attended over twenty different schools, (b) his father was a teacher, (c) he went to an Assembly of God school. ............

2. Tijerina left the migrant stream to (a) form the *Alianza*, (b) establish a village in Arizona, (c) study to become a minister. ............

3. Tijerina learned of the issue of land rights when he (a) entered the Assembly of God school near El Paso, Texas, (b) went to the "Valley of Peace" in Arizona, (c) went to New Mexico. ............

4. After much study, Tijerina became an expert on (a) the Bible, (b) the war between Mexico and the United States, (c) property rights. ............

5. The members of the *Alianza* moved into Kit Carson National forest to (a) arrest the mayor and council members, (b) establish the Republic of San Martín, (c) declare the area the Republic of San Joaquín. ............

6. Members of the *Alianza* raided the courthouse at Tierra Amarilla and tried to (a) free Tijerina from jail, (b) place the district attorney under citizen's arrest, (c) place the district judge under citizen's arrest. ............

7. Tijerina used his trial to (a) draw attention to the issue of police harassment, (b) talk about peace and understanding, (c) draw attention to the land issue. ............

8. After Tijerina got out of jail, he said that (a) the dispute over land rights was not over, (b) he had outgrown militancy, (c) he had been jailed unjustly. ............

# B. VOCABULARY

Match each word in Column A with its meaning in Column B by writing the letter of the meaning in the blank in front of the word.

| | Column A | | Column B |
|---|---|---|---|
| ............ | 1. honor | a. | an attack or to attack |
| ............ | 2. conflict | b. | a person who measures and records the shape of property |
| ............ | 3. issue | c. | to bother by continual attack |
| ............ | 4. surveyor | d. | fight, struggle |
| ............ | 5. incident | e. | subject of disagreement |
| ............ | 6. resentment | f. | an event |
| ............ | 7. confrontation | g. | disagreement |
| ............ | 8. raid | h. | anger caused by a real or imagined injury |
| ............ | 9. harass | i. | meeting of two parties, sometimes accompanied by violence |
| ............ | 10. dispute | j. | to carry out or follow the rules |

# C. THINGS TO TALK ABOUT

Think about the following. Discuss them with your friends or other people you are studying with.

1. Do you think Tijerina had an ability to lead? Give some examples to prove your opinion.

2. What do you think of the methods Tijerina and members of the *Alianza* used for their cause? Can you suggest what can be done for a cause such as theirs?

3. Do you think Tijerina changed after he got out of jail? If you think he did, why do you think this happened?

The University of Texas Information Service

*Collector of Folk Songs*

# Américo Paredes

Américo Paredes is known by many titles—teacher, musician, scholar, and collector of folk songs. He is very proud of all his accomplishments.

Américo was born on September 3, 1915, in Brownsville, Texas. Brownsville is just across the border from Mexico, and the customs of that country are very much a part of the life of the town.

When Américo was young, he learned to play the guitar. He loved to play and sing, and Mexican songs were among his favorites.

Américo also thought of becoming a writer. His parents encouraged him to sing, play, and write.

When he was in high school, Américo won first prize in a statewide poetry contest. He also won a prize for a Spanish essay. Américo graduated as the highest ranking student in his high school class.

Américo then attended Brownsville Junior College. After he graduated, he worked as a newspaper reporter for the Brownsville *Herald*. He also played his guitar and sang songs on his own week-

ly radio program. Soon he was writing songs of his own.

He wrote many poems also. Most of them were published in *La Prensa*, a Mexican American newspaper in San Antonio, Texas. Some of his Spanish poems were published in Mexico.

Américo began writing newspaper articles on folk tales that he had heard when he was a boy. All of the stories were about Mexican Americans living in the Rio Grande Valley.

One day a professor from The University of Texas, Dr. William Owens, came to Brownsville to collect ballads of the Texas border towns. Paredes helped Dr. Owens. He even sang for Owens some ballads that had been in Américo's family for years. The two men talked about the folklore and the folk songs of the Texas-Mexico border. Américo became very interested in collecting folk songs and stories.

When the United States entered World War II, Américo joined the army. He worked as a newspaper reporter for the army newspaper, *Stars and Stripes*.

When Paredes returned to the United States, he decided to leave his work with newspapers for the study of folklore. He entered The University of Texas. While he was in college, he continued to write. He won first prize in two contests, one for a short story he had written and another for his novel, *The Shadow*.

After graduation Américo started teaching part-time at the university and working toward his master's degree. Later, when he began work on his doctor's degree, he decided to do a study of the border songs of the Texas-Mexico border.

Paredes began traveling throughout the Southwest and northern Mexico, collecting songs on his tape recorder. Some forty-seven different singers—men, women, and children—recorded songs for him. He ended up with 361 border songs.

Many of the songs told the stories of raiders, smugglers, and revolutionists from the past. One of the folk ballads was very much like the folk song, "Big Rock Candy Mountain." In "Big Rock Candy Mountain" the singer longs to be at a place where there are mountains made of candy. The Mexican folk ballad tells of streets paved with tamales and mountains made of tortillas.

In 1958 Dr. Paredes published a book, *"With His Pistol in His Hand."* The book deals with a border ballad and its hero, Gregorio Cortez. "El Corrido de Gregorio Cortez" is one of the best-known songs of the Texas-Mexico border. The song is based on an incident that occurred near Kenedy, Texas. In a gunfight between Cortez and Sheriff W. T. Morris, the sheriff was killed. The song deals with the chase, capture, impris-

onment, and eventual pardon of Cortez.

Dr. Paredes has taught at The University of Texas since 1951. He has also lectured at many other schools and for many organizations across the nation. He is the author of eight books and many articles and reviews.

Américo Paredes is proud that he has maintained his identity as a "bicultural citizen of the United States." "Never in my life," he says, "have I abandoned the Spanish language or the Mexican folk culture."

When Dr. Paredes is not writing or teaching, you might find him at home playing his guitar and singing folk songs for his wife, Amelia, and their four children. Wherever he is, folk songs and folk tales are very much a part of Américo Paredes's life.

Paredes collected over 300 border songs with his tape recorder.

## A. UNDERSTANDING THE STORY

Read each of the following carefully. Then select the correct answer from the choices. Write the letter of the correct answer in the blank that follows each.

1. Américo Paredes is all but one of the following: (a) teacher, (b) dancer, (c) musician.   ............

2. When Américo was in high school, he won first place in a (a) song-writing contest, (b) poetry contest, (c) singing contest.   ............

3. Américo graduated from high school as the (a) best poet in the class, (b) best musician in the class, (c) highest ranking student in the class.   ............

4. Américo left his work with newspapers to (a) compose folk songs, (b) enter college, (c) collect pistols.   ............

5. Many of the folk songs Américo collected are (a) not very interesting, (b) about the death of Gregorio Cortez, (c) about raiders, smugglers, and revolutionists.   ............

6. "Big Rock Candy Mountain" is (a) similar to a Mexican folk ballad about streets paved with candy, (b) the English version of the song, "With His Pistol in His Hand," (c) a song about a place with mountains made of candy.   ............

7. "El Corrido de Gregorio Cortez" is (a) a book about the life of Gregorio Cortez, (b) one of the best-known songs of the Texas-Mexico border, (c) a short story about a gunfight.   ............

8. Dr. Paredes says he is proud he has kept his identity as (a) a musician, (b) an artist, (c) a bicultural citizen.   ............

## B. VOCABULARY

Match each word in Column A with its meaning in Column B by writing the letter of the meaning in the blank in front of the word.

| | Column A | | Column B |
|---|---|---|---|
| ............ | 1. contest | a. | a popular song often telling a story |
| ............ | 2. ballad | b. | one who has learned much about a subject |
| ............ | 3. publish | c. | to keep |
| ............ | 4. customs | d. | to give up, to desert |
| ............ | 5. scholar | e. | competition to see who is superior |
| ............ | 6. maintain | f. | to print and distribute to the public |
| ............ | 7. abandon | g. | to feel a desire for something |
| ............ | 8. long (for) | h. | ways of doing things |

## C. THINGS TO WRITE ABOUT

Answer the following questions on the lines provided.

1. Why is the work of Américo Paredes important?

........................................................................................................

........................................................................................................

........................................................................................................

........................................................................................................

........................................................................................................

........................................................................................................

........................................................................................................

2. What is "El Corrido de Gregorio Cortez" about?

........................................................................................................

........................................................................................................

........................................................................................................

........................................................................................................

........................................................................................................

........................................................................................................

........................................................................................................

3. Paredes says he is proud he has not abandoned the Spanish language. Do you think it is a good idea to maintain your language when it is different from that spoken by the majority? Why do you think so?

........................................................................................................

........................................................................................................

........................................................................................................

........................................................................................................

........................................................................................................

........................................................................................................

........................................................................................................

# Manuel Aragón, Jr.

From fruit picker to deputy mayor of the city of Los Angeles—this is the story of the career of Manuel Aragón, Jr. Manuel was born in Los Angeles, California, on August 28, 1931. When he was five, his family moved to Douglas, Arizona. There Manuel's father established his own business.

Later when business conditions became poor, the Aragóns returned to California. The family followed the migrant stream throughout the Santa Clara Valley, picking peaches, walnuts, and prunes. Soon Manuel Aragón, Sr., was offered a job with the U.S. Gypsum Company, and young Manuel dropped out of high school to join his father at the plant.

In 1951 Manuel enlisted in the United States Air Force. He served four years and worked his way up to staff sergeant. After his discharge in 1955, Manuel and his brother Robert entered Los Angeles City College.

Both Manuel and Robert became very involved in student politics at the college. Both men received honors for their academic work, and both served as president of the student body at the college.

Manuel continued his interest in student politics when he enrolled at the University of California at Berkeley. He soon became involved with SLATE. SLATE was a student organization that protested against nuclear testing and racial discrimination.

Manuel ran for student-body president and lost. He also lost valuable time that he needed for his studies. He had been a candidate for honors, but now he was dismissed from the school. However, he entered San Francisco State College and graduated with a degree in economics and political science.

While he was a student at the San Francisco College, Aragón met Corrina Jackson, a student at nearby Mills College. They married in 1960, and now have two children, María and Manolín.

Manuel decided that he wanted to enter the world of business and public service. He joined the Department of Commerce's Economic Development

Manuel Aragón Hosting "Impacto"

Company. He specialized in loans to minority-owned small businesses.

One of the ventures that Aragón enjoyed most was serving as producer and host for "Impacto," a public affairs television program in Los Angeles. The show dealt with the problems of Mexican Americans in the city.

Although Manuel was enjoying a successful career in the fields of public service and business, politics still appealed to him. He actively campaigned with his brothers for John F. Kennedy in 1960. Then the family campaigned for Senator George McGovern when he ran for president of the United States.

When Tom Bradley ran for mayor of the city of Los Angeles in 1973, the Aragóns were among his most active supporters. Bradley became the first black mayor in the history of Los Angeles, and he chose Manuel Aragón to serve as his deputy mayor.

With his background in business and public service, Manuel Aragón represents the entire community in his job. He says he owes all the people "a promise to do the best job as cleanly and honestly as I can."

Administration. Soon he was manager of this forty-million-dollar program.

A few years later, Manuel became the executive director of the Economic and Youth Opportunities Agency of Los Angeles. The agency was in charge of one of the largest anti-poverty programs in the nation. Then Aragón served as president of the City of Commerce Investment

## A. UNDERSTANDING THE STORY

Read each of the following carefully. Then select the correct answer from the choices. Write the letter of the correct answer in the blank that follows each.

1. When Manuel was young, he helped his family (a) work in the fields, (b) run a small restaurant, (c) plan political campaigns. ............

2. Manuel dropped out of school to join his father in (a) entering politics, (b) working in a plant, (c) enlisting in the United States Air Force. ............

3. The first college that Manuel attended was (a) Los Angeles City College, (b) the University of California at Berkeley, (c) San Francisco State College. ............

4. Both Robert and Manuel Aragón (a) earned degrees in economics and political science, (b) were students at San Francisco State College, (c) served as president of the student body of Los Angeles City College. ............

5. After Manuel graduated from college, he decided to enter (a) business and politics, (b) business and public service, (c) public service and politics. ............

6. When Manuel worked for the City of Commerce Investment Company, he specialized in loans to (a) college students, (b) minority-owned small businesses, (c) minority-owned television stations. ............

7. One of the business ventures that Aragón enjoyed most was his work with (a) SLATE, (b) the Economic Development Administration, (c) "Impacto." ............

8. The Aragón family campaigned for (a) John F. Kennedy and Lyndon Johnson, (b) John F. Kennedy and George McGovern, (c) John F. Kennedy and Richard Nixon. ............

9. Manuel Aragón was appointed deputy mayor by (a) George McGovern, (b) Tom Bradley, (c) Corrina Jackson. ............

## B. VOCABULARY

Match each word in Column A with its meaning in Column B by writing the letter of the meaning in the blank in front of the word.

| | Column A | Column B |
|---|---|---|
| ............ | 1. deputy | a. related to schools or education |
| ............ | 2. enlist | b. to ask to leave |
| ............ | 3. throughout | c. to speak out against |
| ............ | 4. career | d. assistant, substitute |
| ............ | 5. academic | e. to work at or study only one thing |
| ............ | 6. dismiss | f. course of action in a person's life |
| ............ | 7. specialize | g. in every part of |
| ............ | 8. protest | h. to join |

# C. THINGS TO WRITE ABOUT

Answer the following questions on the lines provided.

1. Do you think Manuel Aragón's experience and attitude would help to make him a good administrator? Why?

..................................................................................................................
..................................................................................................................
..................................................................................................................
..................................................................................................................
..................................................................................................................
..................................................................................................................

2. Do you think having shows such as "Impacto" is a good idea? Why?

..................................................................................................................
..................................................................................................................
..................................................................................................................
..................................................................................................................
..................................................................................................................
..................................................................................................................

3. How did Manuel Aragón become deputy mayor of Los Angeles?

..................................................................................................................
..................................................................................................................
..................................................................................................................
..................................................................................................................
..................................................................................................................
..................................................................................................................

Freeman and Best, Inc.

*Singer with a Heart*

# Vikki Carr

Vikki Carr's favorite song begins, "I can only give you love that lasts forever; that's all." Vikki says that this is how she feels about life, her friends, and the people who come to hear her sing.

Vikki Carr was born in El Paso, Texas. She was named Florencia Bisenta de Casillas Martínez Cardona. She grew up and went to school in the San Gabriel Valley in California.

The first time Vikki sang in public, she was only four years old. She sang a carol in Latin at a Christmas program.

When Vikki was in high school, she took as many music courses as she could. She played leading roles in the school's musical productions. She also sang on weekends with some of the local bands.

When Vikki graduated, she accepted a job with Pepe Callahan's Mexican-Irish Band. Soon she was singing all the solos. Pepe Callahan thought that "Florencia" was too long a name for a singer. He named her "Carlita." Later, Vikki decided to change her name again. She took "Carr" from her real name of "Cardona" and "Vikki" because she liked it.

Soon Vikki cut her first record. She took her record to various recording companies. Many told her that they could not use her. However, Liberty Records took a chance on her. Soon she was recording hits such as "It Must Be Him" and "Cuando Calienta el Sol," which she sang both in Spanish and in English.

Vikki quickly became a very popular star. She appeared on television with such stars as Dean Martin, Jerry Lewis, Bob Hope, and Carol Burnett. She was also a host on the "Tonight Show."

Vikki performed in several musicals. She appeared in *South Pacific* and later played the lead in *The Unsinkable Molly Brown*. She also took her own show, "The Vikki Carr Show," to London and appeared in a command performance before Queen Elizabeth.

One of her biggest thrills was appearing at the White House. She sang for President Nixon's inauguration and in 1974 opened the Christmas Seal Drive

81

Freeman and Best, Inc.

with President Ford. President Ford later invited her to come to the White House again to sing for the chancellor of Austria.

Vikki has appeared in several dramatic roles on television. However, singing comes first with her. "I love to sing," and I would never give up singing," she says. "I am very grateful for what it's done for me. It's a God-given talent, so I feel I should share it with everybody."

No matter how famous Vikki has become, she never forgets her Mexican American background. She is very proud of her heritage. It wasn't always so. Once, when she was a little girl, she told her father that she thought she must be a Spanish-speaking American. "You are

not," her father replied. "You're a Mexican American."

Vikki has donated both money and time to help Mexican Americans. Once she was asked to do several milk commercials for television. Vikki remembered that when she was young, there often was no milk for the family. She asked that the money she earned from the commercials go to help Mexican Americans.

Another time Vikki was singing at HemisFair in San Antonio, Texas. She heard about a problem at Holy Cross High School. The school was located in the Mexican American section of town. Money was running out, and church officials had decided to move the school to another part of town. Vikki helped raise over fifty thousand dollars to save the school.

In 1971 Vikki organized the Vikki Carr Scholarship Foundation to help needy students go to college. The first year, the foundation helped send eight students to college and the second year nineteen students. Vikki hopes that each year more young people will be sent to college.

Vikki takes a personal interest in all these students. She selects the students herself and keeps up with their progress in school. "I don't have children of my own," Vikki says. "All of these youngsters now in school are like my own family. I couldn't be more proud of what they are doing."

Vikki Carr remembers the advice that her father once gave her when she was discouraged about her career. "Listen to me, dear," her father said. "Not everyone is going to like you. Not everyone is going to like your singing. It is impossible to please them all. Just do your very best and always follow the Golden Rule."

## A. UNDERSTANDING THE STORY

Read each of the following carefully. Then select the correct answer from the choices. Write the letter of the correct answer in the blank that follows each.

1. The first time Vikki sang was (a) with Pepe Callahan's band, (b) in high school, (c) when she was only four years old.  ............

2. The singer's first professional name was (a) Carr, (b) Carlita, (c) Cardona.  ............

3. Vikki appeared in a command performance before (a) Queen Elizabeth, (b) Dean Martin, (c) President Ford.  ............

4. Vikki Carr has been invited to the White House to sing for (a) Presidents Kennedy and Nixon, (b) Queen Elizabeth and the chancellor of Austria, (c) Presidents Nixon and Ford.  ............

5. No matter how famous Vikki has become, she never forgets (a) her family, (b) the first time she sang in public, (c) her Mexican American heritage.  ............

6. Vikki once gave money to help save (a) a poor section of San Antonio, (b) Holy Cross High School, (c) HemisFair.  ............

7. The singer established the (a) HemisFair Foundation, (b) Mexican American Foundation, (c) Vikki Carr Scholarship Foundation.  ............

8. Vikki's father advised her to (a) follow the Golden Rule, (b) give up singing, (c) enter college.  ............

## B. VOCABULARY

The following words were used in the story. Write a short definition for each word that matches its use in the story. Use a dictionary if necessary.

talent ..............................................................................................................

..............................................................................................................

role ..............................................................................................................

..............................................................................................................

progress ..............................................................................................................

..............................................................................................................

needy ..............................................................................................................

..............................................................................................................

foundation ....................................................................................................

....................................................................................................

carol ....................................................................................................

....................................................................................................

discourage ....................................................................................................

....................................................................................................

inauguration ....................................................................................................

....................................................................................................

## C. THINGS TO WRITE ABOUT

Answer the following questions on the lines provided.

1. Do you think Mexican Americans should be proud of the things Vikki Carr has done? Why do you think so?

....................................................................................................

....................................................................................................

....................................................................................................

....................................................................................................

....................................................................................................

....................................................................................................

....................................................................................................

2. Vikki Carr has donated much money and time to help other people. What does this tell you about her personality?

....................................................................................................

....................................................................................................

....................................................................................................

....................................................................................................

....................................................................................................

....................................................................................................

....................................................................................................

# Héctor P. García

When Mexican American soldiers returned to the United States after World War II, they found little appreciation for what they had done. These soldiers, or GIs, had served their country well during the war. They had helped the armed forces achieve victory.

Now they returned to face discrimination. Many found that they could not get jobs or get into the schools and colleges they wanted to attend. The GIs noticed that Mexican Americans who ran for public office rarely won.

Many people began to fight these injustices. One of these was Héctor P. García.

Héctor was born in Mexico on January 17, 1914. His parents, José and Faustina García, were both teachers.

When the family moved to Mercedes, Texas, Héctor's parents saw to it that all their children had a good education. Every day, when the children returned from school, their parents taught them Spanish, Mexican history, and other subjects.

"They made us understand the great-ness of two peoples, the Spaniard and the Aztec Indian," Héctor recalls. "They made us proud of our culture and its greatness."

When Héctor was still in school, his older brother entered medical school and later graduated as a doctor. Encouraged by his brother's accomplishments, Héctor decided to become a doctor.

Héctor attended medical school at The University of Texas and then served his internship in Nebraska. In 1942 he became a doctor.

During World War II, Dr. García joined the army and served in the infantry, engineering, and medical corps. He was awarded a Bronze Star Medal.

While Héctor was serving in Naples, Italy, he met and later married Wanda Fusillo. After the war, the two came to the United States and settled in Corpus Christi, Texas.

It was at this time that Héctor became concerned with discrimination toward Mexican American veterans. He knew he could not solve this problem alone. The GIs had to be organized.

On March 26, 1948, Dr. García and a group of veterans formed the American GI Forum. "We overcame the myth that Mexican Americans could not be organizers," García says.

The Forum was very successful. The organization represented many Mexican Americans in hundreds of court cases and hearings on discrimination. Soon there were GI Forum chapters in over twenty-four states all across the United States.

The Forum has been particularly active in dealing with discrimination in education. "The system has failed in giving the Mexican American educational equality and opportunity," Dr. García says. "The future of Mexican American youth lies on education but more than that on bilingual education and bicultural understanding."

The GI Forum has been an important part of Dr. García's life. He has maintained a private medical practice, but he has been extremely active with the Forum, as well as with other political organizations.

García served as president of PASO, the Political Association of Spanish-speaking Organizations. He also helped the Democratic party in the election of President John F. Kennedy.

President Kennedy appointed Dr. García "special representative" of the United States at a treaty signing in the West Indies. President Johnson also appointed Dr. García to various positions including alternate delegate to the United Nations.

There are many other organizations and committees Dr. García has served on. He has received many awards and recognitions for his work. However, he states, "The founding of the American GI Forum was the greatest achievement I ever undertook."

## A. UNDERSTANDING THE STORY

Read each of the following carefully. Then select the correct answer from the choices. Write the letter of the correct answer in the blank that follows each.

1. After World War II, Mexican American GIs found (a) it easy to obtain jobs, (b) much appreciation for what they had done, (c) much discrimination in this country. ............

2. Héctor's parents taught him (a) how to speak English, (b) Mexican history, (c) to fight against injustice. ............

3. One of the things that encouraged Héctor to become a doctor was the fact that (a) he had a good education, (b) medical school was easy, (c) his brother became a doctor. ...........

4. During the war, Héctor served in the (a) Marine Corps, (b) Medical Corps, (c) navy. ...........

5. Héctor knew that to fight discrimination the GIs had to (a) be organized, (b) enter politics, (c) study law. ...........

6. According to Héctor García, Mexican American youths will have a more promising future if they (a) join the Forum, (b) obtain a good education, (c) organize themselves. ...........

7. Besides his work with the Forum, Dr. García (a) has maintained a private medical practice, (b) has helped form PASO, (c) once served as president of the Democratic party. ...........

8. Héctor says the founding of GI Forum was his (a) greatest achievement, (b) proudest achievement, (c) most difficult achievement. ...........

## B. VOCABULARY

The following words were used in the story. Write a short definition for each word that matches its use in the story. Use a dictionary if necessary.

rarely ............................................................................................................

..........................................................................................................................

settle ............................................................................................................

..........................................................................................................................

concern ............................................................................................................

..........................................................................................................................

hearing ............................................................................................................

..........................................................................................................................

equality ............................................................................................................

..........................................................................................................................

bicultural ............................................................................................................

..........................................................................................................................

forum ............................................................................................................

..........................................................................................................................

treaty ......................................................................................................................

..........................................................................................................................

veteran ...................................................................................................................

..........................................................................................................................

internship ..............................................................................................................

..........................................................................................................................

## C. THINGS TO WRITE ABOUT

Answer the following questions on the lines provided.

1. Héctor's parents helped their children study the Spanish language and Mexican history. How else can parents help their children be proud of their heritage?

..........................................................................................................................

..........................................................................................................................

..........................................................................................................................

..........................................................................................................................

..........................................................................................................................

2. Do you think the veterans had a good idea when they formed the GI Forum?

..........................................................................................................................

..........................................................................................................................

..........................................................................................................................

..........................................................................................................................

3. What does Dr. García mean when he talks about "bicultural understanding"?

..........................................................................................................................

..........................................................................................................................

..........................................................................................................................

..........................................................................................................................

*New Mexico's Senator*

# Joseph Montoya

Joseph Montoya has devoted over forty years of his life to politics and the service of his people. All this time he has worked hard to preserve and improve the rights of the individual.

Joseph Montoya is from one of New Mexico's oldest families. His ancestors settled in the Sandoval County area in the eighteenth century. The Montoyas have lived there ever since. Joseph was born on September 24, 1915, in the small town of Peña Blanca.

Joseph graduated from Bernalillo High School and attended Regis College in Denver. More than anything else, he wanted to be a lawyer. He worked summers and after school to earn the money to enter law school at Georgetown University in Washington, D.C.

When he was twenty-one years old and still in law school, Joseph ran for a seat in the New Mexico House of Representatives. He won his race and became the youngest representative in the state's history.

Later Montoya earned his degree and became a lawyer. When the legislature

met, Montoya served. When the legislature was not in session, he practiced law in Santa Fe, New Mexico. Montoya remained in the state legislature for twelve years as a representative and later as a senator.

However, the young legislator wanted to go to the United States Congress. He served in various state offices until 1957, when he was elected to the United States House of Representatives.

Montoya earned a reputation in Congress for being a dedicated worker. He was known for his work in helping farmers and laborers and for his support of poverty programs.

In 1964 he was elected to fill a term in the United States Senate caused by the death of New Mexico's Senator Dennis Chávez. He has been there ever since.

As a United States senator, Montoya has been helpful in passing bills to fund bilingual education. "Because I understand the importance of education to bicultural citizens, I have done a great deal of work on bilingual and bicultural education," the senator says. "The Mexican American youth of today must have better programs so they can realize and use their heritage." His efforts have drawn the praise of many groups, including the *Alianza Federal de Mercedes* headed by Reies Tijerina.

Montoya has worked to defend the rights of many other groups. He has dealt with such issues as consumer protection, sex discrimination, aid to the elderly, and the plight of New Mexico's Indians.

The New Mexico senator has also worked to help soldiers returning from service in Vietnam. "It is not easy to send our young people to a far-off place to struggle," he says. "Harder still is it to live with the price we must pay. But we can at least try to bind up the wounds they suffer, ease their lot in later life, and give them all a chance to become what they most wish to be."

On February 7, 1973, the Senate of the United States created the Select Committee on Presidential Campaign Activities. The committee studied the issue of presidential campaigns, including Watergate activities. Senator Montoya was one of four Democrats asked to serve on the committee.

As a result of these hearings, Montoya and other senators asked for public financing of federal elections. "Public

Montoya Serving on the Select Committee

financing can move us one step closer toward open, fair, honest elections," the senators stated.

Montoya believes in the idea of self-help. He urges Mexican Americans to educate themselves and become active in government. "Young Mexican Americans must become involved in government to create real change," he says.

Montoya was described by a close friend as "warm-hearted and considerate." The people of New Mexico refer to him affectionately as "Little Joe." Joseph Montoya has a long history of service to the people of his state and to his country.

## A. UNDERSTANDING THE STORY

Read each of the following carefully. Then select the correct answer from the choices. Write the letter of the correct answer in the blank that follows each.

1. Joseph Montoya is from (a) Sandoval City, (b) one of New Mexico's oldest families, (c) Santa Fe. .............

2. More than anything else, Joseph wanted to be a (a) senator, (b) lawyer, (c) legislator. ...........

3. When Montoya was twenty-one, he became New Mexico's (a) youngest member of the House of Representatives, (b) youngest member of the state senate, (c) governor. ...........

4. Montoya is known for his work in (a) helping business leaders, (b) helping farmers and laborers, (c) reducing the funding of poverty programs. ...........

5. According to Montoya, bilingual and bicultural education can help Mexican American youth (a) improve their reading speed, (b) realize and use their heritage, (c) become involved in government. ...........

6. Montoya has defended the rights of the (a) Italians, (b) Chinese, (c) Indians. ...........

7. After serving on the Select Committee on Presidential Campaign Activities, Montoya and other senators (a) decided to retire, (b) asked for a limit on campaign spending, (c) asked for public financing of elections. ...........

8. Montoya believes in the idea of (a) self-help, (b) changing the government, (c) private financing of federal elections. ...........

## B. VOCABULARY

Match each word in Column A with its meaning in Column B by writing the letter of the meaning in the blank in front of the word.

| | Column A | | Column B |
|---|---|---|---|
| ........... | 1. century | a. | with warm regard |
| ........... | 2. reputation | b. | a period of 100 years |
| ........... | 3. dedicated | c. | attracted |
| ........... | 4. drawn | d. | thoughtful of the rights and feelings of others |
| ........... | 5. lot | e. | what people think about a person |
| ........... | 6. preserve | f. | to become aware of |
| ........... | 7. fund | g. | devoted to a cause |
| ........... | 8. realize | h. | state or condition |
| ........... | 9. considerate | i. | to provide money for a cause |
| ........... | 10. affectionately | j. | to protect |

# C. THINGS TO WRITE ABOUT

Answer the following questions on the lines provided.

1. Can you give some examples of how Montoya is concerned for the rights of individuals?

...........................................................................................................

...........................................................................................................

...........................................................................................................

...........................................................................................................

...........................................................................................................

...........................................................................................................

...........................................................................................................

2. How has Senator Montoya helped Mexican Americans?

...........................................................................................................

...........................................................................................................

...........................................................................................................

...........................................................................................................

...........................................................................................................

...........................................................................................................

...........................................................................................................

3. What does Montoya mean when he says that young people must become more involved in government?

...........................................................................................................

...........................................................................................................

...........................................................................................................

...........................................................................................................

...........................................................................................................

...........................................................................................................

*Chicano Bishop*

# Patrick Fernández Flores

On May 5, 1970, a huge crowd of people gathered outside the convention center in San Antonio, Texas. *A mariachi* band played. Men and women chatted with their neighbors. Children ran among the crowd. Signs waved in the breeze. One read, "*¡Viva Nuestro Obispo Chicano!*"

The crowd had gathered to see Father Patrick Flores consecrated as auxiliary bishop of the archdiocese of San Antonio. Bishop Flores had become, at the age of forty, one of the youngest men ever to be named bishop and at that time the only Mexican American bishop in the United States.

A man in the clothes of a farm worker stood to read the Epistle. He was César Chávez, the man Bishop Flores had marched beside, and the man many people compared Flores with.

Bishop Flores is a spirited and aggressive leader. He often counsels the poor and the uneducated to not accept their lot in life. "People must not be victims," he says.

Patrick Flores was born on July 26, 1929, in Ganado, Texas. He was the seventh of nine children born to Patricio and Trinidad Fernández Flores. His parents were migrant workers, and Patrick spent much of his time working in the fields.

Flores often encountered prejudice and discrimination when he was young. He knew how it felt not to be allowed to go to swimming pools, ice-cream parlors, or theaters.

Because his family was constantly moving, Patrick never went to school for more than four or five months out of each year. When his father earned enough money to buy a small farm, Patrick dropped out of high school to help. While he was working in the fields, he dreamed of becoming a priest.

Local priests did not encourage the young boy to follow this vocation. Some people thought he had promise, but they thought he should try for a career in law or medicine.

A nun believed that young Patrick had a true religious vocation and took the boy to the bishop in Galveston. The

93

Flores often has mariachis play at his masses.

bishop offered to help Patrick finish high school.

At the age of twenty, Patrick Flores graduated from high school—at the head of his class. He entered St. Mary's Seminary to study for the priesthood. When he was ordained, he became one of two Chicano priests in the Houston-Galveston diocese.

Father Flores immediately became involved in the social, political, and spiritual life of his community. He was a very popular priest, known for offering mass with *mariachi* music.

Now as a bishop, Flores continues to work with the people he considers "society's victims." He marches beside striking workers; counsels families left homeless by disasters; and goes into the *barrios*, the fields, and the factories to help the poor. He helps people register for food stamps or welfare programs. He often testifies for people in court or visits them in jail. He preaches the doctrine that Christ came to us to make people free—not only free from sin, but free from poverty, disease, hunger, ignorance, and injustice.

"A priest must understand the culture, the language, and the emotions of the people," Bishop Flores says. "Keeping in touch" is very much a part of the bishop's life.

"Mexicans have a lot of parties, anniversaries, and baptisms," he says. "I try to go to as many as possible. I get to know people. When people are at home is when they want to tell you their problems."

Bishop Flores speaks out loudly and firmly in support of a better way of living for all. He works for better health facilities and better housing. He is also concerned that people obtain good jobs and adequate pay.

In 1972 workers struck against a large clothing manufacturing company. Bishop Flores supported their cause. "Workers must seek the support of the unions to better their conditions in life," Flores said.

Bishop Flores is a man who strives for justice for all people, rich and poor. One day he heard of the plight of Aureliano Silva. Silva was being tried for a crime many people said he didn't commit, and he had no money for his defense. Father Antonio Marranón, Silva's priest, received a package with the bishop's ring and the message, "You must use this ring for Aureliano Silva's defense."

Bishop Flores suggested that the ring be raffled. People bought tickets at two dollars each, and on Christmas Eve the ring was raffled. The winning ticket had

Bishop Flores Visiting Farm Workers

the name Aureliano Silva on it. People had bought tickets and signed the names of Silva or Bishop Flores rather than their own.

The Silva family had money for Aureliano's defense, and they had Bishop Flores's ring. They returned the ring to the bishop. Before Bishop Flores would wear the ring again, he took it to a jeweler. Inside the ring he had inscribed —*Recuerdo de Aureliano Silva*, "In memory of Aureliano Silva."

## A. UNDERSTANDING THE STORY

Read each of the following carefully. Then select the correct answer from the choices. Write the letter of the correct answer in the blank that follows each.

1. People gathered outside the San Antonio convention center to (a) celebrate a fiesta, (b) listen to a *mariachi* band, (c) see Father Flores consecrated. ............

2. At the time of his consecration, Bishop Flores became (a) one of two Mexican American bishops in the United States, (b) the only Mexican American bishop in this country, (c) one of several Mexican American bishops in the United States. ............

3. Bishop Flores counsels the poor to (a) accept their lot in life (b) become victims, (c) not accept their lot in life. ............

4. When Flores was young, he (a) experienced discrimination, (b) led a good life, (c) had adequate schooling. ............

5. When young Patrick expressed a desire to become a priest, local priests (a) encouraged him to try, (b) took the boy to the bishop, (c) did not encourage him. ............

6. Since becoming a bishop, Patrick Flores has not (a) been able to attend many celebrations, (b) lost contact with people, (c) kept in touch. ............

7. Bishop Flores struggles and hopes for (a) a better life for all, (b) more fiestas for Mexican Americans, (c) spiritual matters only. ............

8. Bishop Flores is a man who (a) opposes unions, (b) strives for justice, (c) believes problems will solve themselves if people don't interfere. ............

9. Flores helped the Silva family by (a) praying for them, (b) giving them his ring to sell, (c) providing his ring for a raffle to raise money for Silva's defense. ............

# B. VOCABULARY

Match each word in Column A with the meaning in Column B by writing the letter of the meaning in the blank in front of the word.

| | Column A | | Column B |
|---|---|---|---|
| ............ | 1. chatted | a. | to give advice |
| ............ | 2. spirited | b. | something built or established to serve some function |
| ............ | 3. aggressive | c. | good enough, sufficient |
| ............ | 4. counsel | d. | bad situation |
| ............ | 5. encounter | e. | occupied with |
| ............ | 6. involved | f. | bold, ready to fight |
| ............ | 7. adequate | g. | to struggle for something |
| ............ | 8. facility | h. | lively, full of vigor |
| ............ | 9. strive | i. | to come upon |
| ............ | 10. plight | j. | talked |

# C. THINGS TO TALK ABOUT

Think about the following. Discuss them with your friends or other people you are studying with.

1. Why do you think Mexican Americans were so happy at the consecration of Bishop Flores? Why are members of any minority group happy when one of their members reaches a high position?

2. What does Bishop Flores mean when he says, "People must not be victims"?

3. Do you agree with Bishop Flores when he says, "A priest must understand the culture, the language, and the emotions of the people"?

4. Do you think Bishop Flores is truly concerned with people? Explain.

# ANSWER KEY

**Page 3**
**A.** 1. c, 2. b, 3. b, 4. c, 5. a, 6. c, 7. b, 8. a,

**Page 4**
9. b, 10. c. **B.** 1. c, 2. i, 3. g, 4. b, 5. e, 6. h, 7. f, 8. a, 9. j, 10. d. **C.** *Questions are for discussion purposes only.*

**Page 7**
**A.** 1. b, 2. c, 3. b, 4. a, 5. c, 6. a, 7. a, 8. c. **B.** (Part 1) *Definitions may vary. Suggested: challenge*—to call to take part in a fight or contest, to dare; *minority*—a small group of people of a different race, religion, etc.; *disappointment*—an unsatisfying feeling from not receiving or achieving what was expected; *guideline*—an outline of policy or conduct;

**Page 8**
*appeal*—to be interesting or attractive; *ethnic*—of or related to race; *caucus*—a closed meeting of a group of people belonging to the same political party or faction usually to select candidates or decide on policy; *hesitate*—to stop or pause because of doubt; (Part 2) con-vento—convent, sacrificar—sacrifice, realizar—realize, communidad—community, dedicar—dedicate. **C.** *Questions are for discussion purposes only.*

**Page 10**
A. 1. b,

**Page 11**
2. c, 3. a, 4. c, 5. b, 6. b, 7. a, 8. a. **B.** 1. traveler—tourist, 2. fashion—style, 3. surroundings—atmosphere, 4. entertain—amuse, 5. hall—auditorium, 6. chance—opportunity, 7. assemble—gather, 8. steal—rustle, 9. judgment—sentence.

**Page 12**
**C.** *Answers will vary.*

**Page 15**
**A.** 1. b, 2. b, 3. c, 4. b, 5. c, 6. a, 7. c, 8. a, 9. a, 10. b.

**Page 16**
**B.** 1. e, 2. g, 3. f, 4. h, 5. a, 6. d, 7. i, 8. b, 9. j, 10. c. **C.** *Questions are for discussion purposes only.*

**Page 19**
**A.** 1. c, 2. b, 3. c, 4. c, 5. b, 6. a, 7. b, 8. a. **B.** *Definitions may vary. Suggested: ballot*—a written or printed form used in secret voting; *discrimination*—prejudiced outlook, action, or treatment; *identity*—who a person is; *filibuster*—the act of preventing certain legislative action by delaying tactics;

**Page 20**
*segregation*—the isolation or separation of a race, class, or ethnic group from the majority group; *commerce*—the buying and selling of goods; *schedule*—a list of the times when certain things are to happen; *uphold*—to agree with, to support. **C.** *Answers will vary.*

**Page 22**
**A.** 1. b,

**Page 23**
2. c, 3. a, 4. b, 5. c, 6. b, 7. c, 8. a. **B.** 1. advantages—benefits, 2. refused—denied, 3. establish—set, 4. give—provide, 5. situation—condition, 6. rich—wealthy, 7. portion—share, 8. affect—inspire.

**Page 24**
**C.** *Answers will vary.*

**Page 26**
**A.** 1. c,

**Page 27**
2. c, 3. b, 4. b, 5. b, 6. b, 7. c, 8. a. **B.**

97

1. e, 2. g, 3. i, 4. a, 5. h, 6. b, 7. c, 8. d, 9. j, 10. f.

**Page 28**
**C.** *Answers will vary.*

**Page 31**
**A.** 1. c, 2. c, 3. b, 4. c, 5. a, 6. a, 7. c, 8. b, 9. a.

**Page 32**
**B.** 1. awful—splendid, 2. rough—smooth, 3. excludes—includes, 4. unknown—famous, 5. destroy—create, 6. repress—express, 7. sadness—joy, 8. denied—granted. **C.** *Questions are for discussion purposes only.*

**Page 35**
**A.** 1. c, 2. c, 3. c, 4. a, 5. b, 6. b, 7. c, 8. c.

**Page 36**
**B.** (Part 1) 1. d, 2. f, 3. j, 4. g, 5. b, 6. h, 7. c, 8. e, 9. a, 10. i, (Part 2) influencia—influence, revolución—revolution, tumulto—turmoil, organizar—organize, militante—militant. **C.** *Questions are for discussion purposes only.*

**Page 39**
**A.** 1. c, 2. b, 3. b, 4. a, 5. a, 6. b, 7. b, 8. a. **B.** *Definitions may vary. Suggested: surety bond*—a bond guaranteeing performance of a contract or obligation; *fierce*—violent, intense; *reform*—improvements, change for the better; *playwright*—a person who writes plays;

**Page 40**
*crusade*—any campaign for reform or improvement; *amateur*—a person who takes part in some activity for pleasure and not for money; *associate*—to connect in thought; *epic*—a long, serious poem about a hero or heroes; *isolation*—setting apart from others; *controversial*—likely to cause disagreement. **C.** *Questions are for discussion purposes only.*

**Page 42**
**A.** 1. b,

**Page 43**
2. c, 3. b, 4. c, 5. c, 6. b, 7. a, 8. c. **B.** 1. large—huge, 2. pleasant—comfortable, 3. ghetto—slum, 4. gain—earn, 5. chief—leading, 6. rugged—tough, 7. respect—admire, 8. well-liked—popular, 9. prepare—arrange.

**Page 44**
**C.** *Answers will vary.*

**Page 46**
**A.** 1. c,

**Page 47**
2. c, 3. c, 4. c, 5. a, 6. c, 7. a, 8. b. **B.** 1. c, 2. h, 3. e, 4. f, 5. g, 6. j, 7. b, 8. d, 9. a, 10. i.

**Page 48**
**C.** *Answers will vary.*

**Page 50**
**A.** 1. c,

**Page 51**
2. a, 3. b, 4. c, 5. a, 6. b, 7. b, 8. b. **B.** 1. rejected—accepted, 2. advantage—handicap, 3. success—failure, 4. repulsion—desire, 5. disappointed—pleased, 6. always—seldom, 7. disrespect—respect, 8. unjust—fair.

**Page 52**
**C.** *Answers will vary.*

**Page 54**
**A.** 1. b, 2. c, 3. a,

**Page 55**
4. c, 5. b, 6. b, 7. c, 8. b. **B.** *Definitions may vary. Suggested: ancestor*—a person from whom one is directly decended; *meager*—small; *originate*—to start; *supplement*—to make addition to, to complete; *afford*—to have enough money or time to spare for; *vow*—a solemn promise; *candidate*—a person

running for office; *monitor*—to listen or watch in order to check up on.

## Page 56
**C.** *Answers will vary.*

## Page 59
**A.** 1. b, 2. a, 3. c, 4. a, 5. b, 6. c, 7. c, 8. c. **B.** 1. cover—wrap, 2. solitary—lonely, 3. announcement—notice, 4. decline—slump, 5. gamble—risk, 6. screams—roars, 7. classify—rank, 8. obligations—duties.

## Page 60
**C.** *Answers will vary.*

## Page 62
**A.** 1. c,

## Page 63
2. a, 3. b, 4. c, 5. b, 6. b, 7. a, 8. b. **B.** *Definitions may vary. Suggested: basic*—fundamental, serving as the basis or starting point; *cycle*—a series of events that takes place over and over again; *rewarding*—satisfying; *quest*—search; *authority*—a person who is an expert on a particular subject;

## Page 64
*semester*—one of the terms that make up a school year; *scholarship*—money given to a student to help continue his or her education; *vocal*—speaking often and openly; *financial*—having to do with money matters; *responsibility*—that for which one is answerable, duty or trust. **C.** *Answers will vary.*

## Page 67
**A.** 1. c, 2. b, 3. b, 4. c, 5. b, 6. b, 7. c, 8. b, 9. a.

## Page 68
**B.** (Part 1) 1. h, 2. g, 3. a, 4. b, 5. j, 6. d, 7. c, 8. f, 9. e, 10. i, (Part 2) asesinar—assassinate, apreciar—appreciate, fascinar—fascinate, hábito—habit, reconocer—recognize. **C.** *Questions are for discussion purposes only.*

## Page 71
**A.** 1. a, 2. c, 3. c, 4. c, 5. c, 6. b, 7. c, 8. b.

## Page 72
**B.** 1. j, 2. d, 3. e, 4. b, 5. f, 6. h, 7. i, 8. a, 9. c, 10. g. **C.** *Questions are for discussion purposes only.*

## Page 75
**A.** 1. b, 2. b, 3. c, 4. b, 5. c, 6. c, 7. b, 8. c. **B.** 1. e, 2. a, 3. f, 4. h, 5. b, 6. c, 7. d, 8. g.

## Page 76
**C.** *Answers will vary.*

## Page 78
**A.** 1. a, 2. b,

## Page 79
3. a, 4. c, 5. b, 6. b, 7. c, 8. b, 9. b. **B.** 1. d, 2. h, 3. g, 4. f, 5. a, 6. b, 7. e, 8. c.

## Page 80
**C.** *Answers will vary.*

## Page 83
**A.** 1. c, 2. b, 3. a, 4. c, 5. c, 6. b, 7. c, 8. a. **B.** *Definitions may vary. Suggested: talent*—a special ability; *role*—part or character taken in a play; *progress*—development, improvement; *needy*—very poor;

## Page 84
*foundation*—a fund set up for helping people in certain endeavors; *carol*—a song of joy or praise; *discourage*—to cause to lose hope or confidence; *inauguration*—a ceremonial induction into office. **C.** *Answers will vary.*

## Page 86
**A.** 1. c, 2. b,

## Page 87
3. c, 4. b, 5. a, 6. b, 7. a, 8. a. **B.** *Definitions may vary. Suggested: rarely*—not very often, hardly ever; *settle*—to make one's home; *concern*—anxious interest; *hearing*—a session (such as in a court)

where witnesses are heard and testimony is taken; *equality*—the state of being equal, especially having the same political and social rights; *bicultural*—related to two cultures; *forum*—a public meeting;

**Page 88**
*treaty*—a formal agreement between two parties; *veteran*—a person who has served in the armed forces; *internship*—a training period in actual service as an employee. **C.** *Answers will vary.*

**Page 90**
**A.** 1. b,

**Page 91**
2. b, 3. a, 4. b, 5. b, 6. c, 7. c, 8. a. **B.** 1. b, 2. e, 3. g, 4. c, 5. h, 6. j, 7. i, 8. f, 9. d, 10. a.

**Page 92**
**C.** *Answers will vary.*

**Page 95**
**A.** 1. c, 2. b, 3. c, 4. a, 5. c, 6. b, 7. a, 8. b, 9. c.

**Page 96**
**B.** 1. j, 2. h, 3. f, 4. a, 5. i, 6. e, 7. c, 8. b, 9. g, 10. d. **C.** *Questions are for discussion purposes only.*